Be ALL You Could Be...

# Be ALL You Could Be...

*Restoring Hope and Creating Vision for the
Stunted Christian Camp*

by
Earl Taylor

*Foreword by Bob Kobielush*

Be ALL You Could Be

Cover design by: Emily Delia Fay

# Preface

*This is written for the stunted camp: the camp with just a handful of staff members who are over worked, underpaid, and in need of advice and hope. This is written for the new guy just fresh from another career who has been called from his layman's job into the camping ministry; there has been no training, no schooling.*

*I pray that my stories will give you hope. I pray that you take my advice and apply some part of the principles that I lay out. I pray you make it through your first year or your fifth year or your fiftieth year rejoicing in the faithfulness of God: Jehovah-jireh, our Provider, our Helper, our Guide.*

*Extra large camps don't need this advice; they lead the seminars. But, if by chance you read this, I pray it will light a spark in your heart and give you opportunities to remember on whose shoulders you are standing today.*

*We are grateful for the pioneers, the visionaries, the faithful laborers for the cause of Christ through Christian camping in the United States and abroad. I often reflect on Bob Kobielush and am thankful for his wise advice of blending ministry and business principles*

*through his own newsletters to us rookie-type direc-*
*tors while he was leading our Christian Camping and*
*Conference Association.*

# Dedication

Dedicated to my dad,
Waylon E. Taylor— 1928-2008,
an ardent supporter of the little guy, the weary, the
faithful who needed an
extra hand of encouragement and love.

My prayer is that this book will bring hope to you
as I saw my dad do so often in his ministry—
by "putting wind behind so many people's sails"
through his love and encouragement.

# Table of Contents

# Foreword in a Nutshell

Here is a straight-forward and highly informative book that must be read by those who are serious participants in, or looking at involvement with, a Christian camp, conference or retreat center. Based on his success of growing a camp from 80 to 880 beds over 29 years, Earl Taylor gives you leadership and management gems of wisdom that only can be articulated by someone who has been there. AND he says it in a no-nonsense, forthright manner that jolts, resonates and may even cause you to chuckle--refreshing, insightful, gutsy, and down-right practical. I highly recommend this book to novice and veteran alike, no matter what the type or size of your camp. Here's an excellent resource that cuts through the rhetoric for the reader and could also be used to stimulate great group discussions. Thank you, Earl, for this unique gift!

*Bob Kobielush*

Former President of
Christian Camp and Conference Association
(*previously CCI/USA*)

# Foreword Elaborated

Earl Taylor, and the select few who attempt to do what he does, is the reason I gave more than 38 years of my full-time professional ministry to work with and serve Christian camp, conference and retreat center leaders. They are a unique bunch!

They come from all walks of life, look and act in different ways, but all share a persuasively passionate desire to serve people (young, old and everyone in between) through the unique power of the Christian camp, conference and retreat center experience. In these environments countless thousands annually meet their Savior, Jesus Christ, and grow in their Christian understanding and commitment. Here participants create memories and discover Godly behavior that shapes them for a lifetime... and I am not kidding. Many of you know of which I speak. These "end products" of a Christian camping experience fill our pulpits, traverse the globe with a cup of cold water in Jesus' name, walk the halls and fill the chambers of government and corporations alike, nurture our children, and fill the world with Christ's everlasting love and perspectives that were born at a Christian camp.

To produce these results the Earl Taylors of the world provide one of the most unique and powerful environments ever discovered to evangelize and produce disciples in the Kingdom of God. Here, for a relatively short period of time (a week or so, or even a week-end) a 24/7 temporary community is created and infused with the Gospel of Jesus Christ. His message is not only heard but seen in the lives of those who serve. This pregnant environment produces changed lives—forever.

To the casual observer and veteran camp leader, alike, the end result is what matters. However, known only to the veteran camping leader, is the downright all-consuming skill and commitment that is needed to produce these results. To be successful the leader of these ministries must effectively know finances, programming, marketing, sales, food service, health care, risk management, government regulations, construction, maintenance, human resources, theology, educational principles, sewers, strategic planning, security, board relations, environmental care, site development, and, oh yes, speaking, technology, and how to openly laugh and cry... to cite a few qualifications. These leaders are like city managers who not only provide the infrastructure, but also all the day to day goods and services necessary to make life safe, comfortable and exciting for all who occupy these hallowed grounds for a short period of time.

To survive and thrive, camp leadership borrows principles and understandings from dozens of related fields and then applies them often in unique and unorthodox ways. So in these pages you get a good look at what it takes, through the eyes of a successful veteran, Earl Taylor, to manage and lead a Christian camp to success. While many attempt to do what he does, hardly any take the time, or have the talent, to write a book that helps others to successfully lead in these ministries.

In this book you will find practical advice that cuts through the fog of philosophy, and tells you what it really takes to be successful in growing and running a Christian camp, conference or retreat center. Yet, to the observing eye, you will soon realize that the "how to" is grounded in good thinking and philosophy via a quote from a book or well-known leader.

Instead of giving you scriptural "proof texting" throughout, each chapter ends with a Scriptural verse or two setting the whole idea within a Christian context. I find this refreshing rather than distracting from the focus of the text with verses of Scripture throughout. Further, at the end of each chapter there are "Points to Ponder". This not only has individual value, but I believe makes the book a great resource for discussions with staff, boards, volunteers, students, or any serious group pursuing success in these ministries.

Again, thank you Earl for sharing your experiential insights and wisdom with us. I not only appreciate the good content, but the candid ways in which you express these truths. This is helpful and refreshing!

*Bob Kobielush*

## CHAPTER 1

# Steps to Revitalizing a Stunted Camp

I have been intrigued by the Scott Hamilton story: Scott Hamilton, the 1984 Olympic figure skating champion. Early in his life, his adopted parents recognized that he was not growing; they went from specialist to specialist trying to solve the mystery of why his frame was not keeping up with his age. There were no answers, but his doctors did recommend exercise and good nutrition. His parents chose ice skating as his form of exercise– and the rest is history.

Fast forward 20 years to 2004. Scott had already become the most celebrated Olympic ice skater in the United States; he was beloved by everyone— he had captured our hearts. He was retired from the ice, a cancer survivor, married, with one small son–when he came home and told his wife, "I have a brain tumor." Biopsies were taken. Surgery was performed. It turned out that his tumor had been there from the time of his birth– after 44 years, they finally found the reason for his growth being stunted. The mystery of his lack of growth was solved.

Many of you in Christian camping might be asking the same question as Scott's parents did when they asked, "Why is Scott stunted? What is going on that is not allowing him to grow into being full-sized?" But, instead of a child, it is your camp and you too are wondering, "Why are we stunted? We have all the components of a camp: buildings, land, location, recreation— we should be bigger than we are. We should be growing. We should be influencing more people with the Gospel. We feel stunted."

But right now, you are unable to see the "tumor" that is keeping you from growing into the camp that you want to become. Perhaps in this book you will gain some new understanding of what is going on internally that keeps you from growing externally. I trust we will find the cause.

*Another sports story:* I love wrestling: I wrestled; my son wrestled; my dad loved wrestling. I prefer to use the wrestling match as my metaphor as I attempt to describe the camp who is stunted– stagnant– stalled; a camp who appears to be lying on the mat facing the lights of the gym. Down— but not out. The important thing to remember— the match is not over.

Countless times I have seen my son, the wrestler, return from the on-his-back position to the standing-on-his-feet position, having recovered from his mistake of letting down his guard or lack of focus. Once back on his feet, he becomes revitalized, more determined, and has more energy and vitality. He comes out victorious over his opponent with a series of strategic moves- eventually pinning his foe to the mat; he moves from being immobilized to becoming the attacker— the one who is in control! He changed his position with strategy. He changed his position with a plan and technique. He changed his position by will-power and determination. He out-thought the opponent. He renewed his mind; he became the "I can" person instead of the "I can't" person. Strength and stamina are restored. His movements are accelerated. He is alive again. Hope floats!

Once he has his first victory in a tournament he has momentum... and momentum lifts him into the finals. From then on, life is the finals.

Nothing brings life to the crowd faster than a close match or a come-back-from-behind performance by a team; we see it in wrestling, in basketball, in football, and in all sports.

Camps do have the team image: the board (representing the owner); the director (coach); the staff (players); and the guests (fans) have to be knitted together into a complete unit. There has to be victories by the team, or the fans stop attending the games. The coach has to lead with a steady, firm hand, but can't micromanage the players until they don't know their positions or their routine. The owner has to provide the equipment and the facilities or the staff is unable to win. If all four components are functioning together properly- the team is propelled forward for more victories, more growth, with even more fans right to the top- to a super bowl-like experience! Winning: a.k.a. sustainability, is everything regardless of the size or scope of a ministry.

However the sports analogy breaks down when it comes to the mission: sports teams want prestige; *camping ministries want to populate heaven.*

I know of camps with 100 beds that play like they are in big leagues: they consistently score high marks with their churches and their guests; they know how to do camp for 100 to the highest level. They have the service, the hospitality, the beds, the plates, the administration, and the facility operating with efficiency and profitability.

I know of camps with 1000 beds that **look** like they **should** be a major league team– but they play like they are a high school junior varsity girls softball team. Their churches and guests have stopped trusting them to get it right: there is debt, staff fighting, poor food, unclean bedrooms, unsteady and confused administration, buildings that need maintenance, and a poor cash flow to boot. They are operating this 1000 bed facility inefficiently and unprofitably.

Not all camp boards want their camp to be the extra large camp with 1000 beds. Some boards wants their camp to be the 150 bed camp that meets the particular needs of a group of churches, and does it well, with excellence in service and programs, with financial solvency. I saw this when I visited Camp of the Hills near Marble Falls, Texas. Everywhere I looked, I saw great things happening at the camp; there was energy, life, and a large group of volunteers pouring their service into the life of the camp. They knew their mission was to reach under-privileged children; they did it very well.

This is a key issue that needs to be determined by the director and the board. The two must be in sync about the actual size of the camp. They have to agree upon the quality (level of service and facilities) of the camp. Some camps want to offer Motel 6 service, while others settle in with Best Western service, and some strive to be Ritz-Carlton-like in as many shapes and forms as possible.

When the board and the director cannot agree on these two issues— the quality of services and the number of beds that are to be developed and maintained— you have a wrong fit. You have two rails that cannot be used for a train to travel on: you have a wreck.

Let's follow the train track analogy a bit further. Two rails: one the board and one the director; both heading in a unified direction. It makes for smooth traveling by the rest of the staff. Each staff can sit in their own car (job description) and know where their efforts are taking them. The guests can easily ride in the caboose, cheering on the rest of the train— supporting, cheerleading, and utilizing all the efforts of those in front of them: great summer camp program, outstanding retreat facilities combined with great service and warm hospitality.

Many camps are stunted or perhaps even retreating for this very reason: misaligned expectations between the board and the director. Their rails are not parallel.

## The word stunted describes a condition and not a position!

A camp can move from a weak condition to a strong condition without moving from its current size: the camp just matures internally from a visionless organization to one with vision and purpose. It refines systems, creates comfortable facilities and offers the best food and beds possible. When a camp does this, they can be guaranteed the life of the camp will remain vital and significant. It could mean they will grow into a larger size of camp. Much of that depends of the size of constituency, the location in relation to a large population of potential users, and the desire of the board to want to enlarge.

It's the director's responsibility to mature the operations of the camp to its highest quality level possible; it is for the camp board to decide if they want numerical growth. It is the director's role to position the camp in a place of taking the next step to the next level: the board will have to either agree or disagree and then release the director to build even bigger or to set a cap on the growth limits.

Many boards are more than pleased just to have a great camp that will serve their people in the best fashion possible, without investing more capital into more buildings. It takes more buildings and more beds for a camp to grow significantly.

We added a 40 bed lodge recently to our camp. We increased the yearly retreat revenue by $50,000 per year. This new lodge costs the camp $16,000 a year to operate- thus a $34,000 profit, which was turned into another full time staff member, which allowed more personnel to create more programs, which will draw more people to attend, which will mean there will be the need for more buildings and beds, which will mean more revenue... and the cycle goes on until the camp not only has enlarged its influence, it has created so much momentum that it is nearly impossible to stop. It has created sustainability.

How do you make a stalled, stunted camp into a vibrant camp? I could say just add more beds; but I can't say JUST that. If you are an older camp with buildings with some physical challenges— these challenges have to be overcome with visual updates: remodeling, reconfiguration, and re-thinking of programs that can utilize these older buildings. You need your face lifted, your belly tucked, and you simply need to put on some make-up!

As part of revitalizing a stunted camp, the old must become new; the stink must become odor free; the beds have to move from hard and lumpy to comfortable and cozy; the food has to move from blah/boring/summer camp food to colorful, nutritious food that is adult friendly and presented well. The entire camp has to move together toward revitalizing. Creating great beds without great food equals unmet expectations. Creating great food and keeping the bad mattresses causes tired/grumpy guests. Well-rested, well-fed guests return to camp next year, reducing dollars and time spent on marketing. This, in turn, allows the marketing dollars to move to program development and program development means more and more fun things to do while attending camp and sleeping in comfortable beds and eating great food.

This is synergy.
This is a well oiled machine.
This is congruent management.
This is all cylinders clicking.

*This is fun!*

## *Points to Ponder*

1. Are we as a camp considered a well-oiled machine, or do we rattle, sputter, and back-fire? Why?

2. Do our leadership and board run on the same track in the same direction? Why not? What will it take for both to be in sync with each other?

3. How would you describe our camp— vibrant and growing or stalled and stunted?

4. Do we as a camp staff want to create momentum? How committed are we to doing the things necessary to create victories?

5. What are some steps we can take to get all four parts of the team playing with efficiency and purpose?

*Do two walk together*
*unless they have agreed to meet?*

*Amos 3:3*

## Chapter 2
# Everything Rises and Falls on Leadership

In his book, *The 21 Irrefutable Laws of Leadership*, John Maxwell writes that "everything rises and falls on leadership." If Maxwell's statement is accurate, it can really be tested in our camps. Which is to say— "every camp can be either a success or a failure depending on whether it has the right or the wrong leader."

What makes the right leader? Is there a formula that guarantees that a newly hired director of the camp is the right person? I have seen loud leaders lead well. I have seen quiet leaders lead well. I have seen happy-go-lucky leaders be successful. I have seen serious, thoughtful leaders lead well. But regardless of style, personality, and technical skills— it still has to be the right fit. The director's performance and attitudes must meet the board's expectations.

Here is a list of at least eight different kinds of camp directors:

- **The Handyman**- They are more comfortable with a hammer and saw, but are always warm and friendly. They usually are a good listener and a compassionate person. They love the camp, but they hate the office life; they will only stop by the office to clean off their desk of messages and sign some letters. They are very content letting the office staff run the administration of the camp.

- **The Bean Counter**- This director loves their desk and loves numbers and figures. They love filing information: policies and procedures. They love insignificant details and love to create charts of the details. They love profit and loss statements. They are not a creative thinker, and would much rather read about what others are doing, than dream up something new.

- **The Visionary**- They never sits still and they never finish a project before they are on to their next one. The more projects going on at the same time the better. They love watching and directing as others fulfill their dreams. They must have others to connect the dots and to pick up and finish projects which they start. Their staff has a hard time keeping up with them and at times their staff can become frustrated; they are a doer and a driver.

- **The Happy One**- This director just loves to go around hugging and loving on people. They thrive on personal contact. They are a wonderful promoter. Hospitality is their specialty and they love to make people feel special. They are great on ideas, but can be weak with execution. They do not like confrontation. They direct by a consensus of staff rather than from a position of authority.

- **The Jack of all Trades**- This director can sit in their office, but only if there are tasks to do. They love the building and planning of buildings, they love operating the equipment, they love to be with people, they love to see everyone busy, and they love good efficient systems that are smooth and seamless. They are comfortable in the kitchen, the maintenance shop, and working along-side guest services. They can do it all and are very happy helping others.

- **The Administrator**- They love paper, projects, people, and progress. They are an aggressive business type— the true-blue CEO. They are more comfortable in a suit than overalls. They love productive meetings. They love meeting clients. They know finance. They talk big finance and investment talk comfortably. They enjoy fund raising. They know little of the nuts and bolts of the operation— and don't care to know. They are not interested in program, but knows it is necessary. They thrive on the business side of camp.

- **The Program Guy**- They want to have fun, to hang out with staff and plan the next big event. They are great with video and audio equipment. They were once a youth pastor who was an exorbitant planner— but not so great at implementation. They are known to run by the seat of his pants. They are very creative, energetic, and a fun person to have for the boss; but they usually are more people oriented than project oriented– they don't understand maintenance or new construction.

- **The Preacher**- They are a great speaker, Bible teacher and encourager to the staff. They are very strong on church visits, pastor relations, and can be a good fund raiser. They are usually a good listener and enjoy theological conversations with others. They are usually not interested in the mechanical side of camp– the maintenance building. They can be a bit unpractical at times. They have a hard time being involved in the day-to-day operation.

Which one of the eight would be the right fit for the actual jobs that are required of the director? Give up? That's just the problem. Not one type of person fits all. The smaller the camp, the more multi-talented the director needs to be. Extra large camps have the luxury of hiring a specific type of director according to their perceived needs– usually the Administrator; they have a large staff to pick up the other seven roles. Small camp directors are to be a blend of all eight.

If Maxwell is correct: "Everything rises and falls on leadership," then getting the right person to fill a director's position is key for the success or the failure of the camp. The right director: with the needed leadership skills can single handedly take a camp and mature it and be successful– whether small, medium, large or extra large. The opposite is also true: the wrong director with the wrong leadership skills can take the small, medium, large, or extra large camp and kill it; or at least badly wound it.

It will either rise or it will fall.

I have been the director of a camp for 27 years. When I started as the director, I had no training as a director. I was trained to be an English teacher, who ended up being a grounds keeper/maintenance man for seven years at two separate camps before I was asked to be the interim director. I replaced the director who had been with the camp for six years.

The camp was small and had two other staff members besides myself: a secretary/registrar, and a maintenance/grounds keeper. We hired some part-time cooks during the retreat season. I did the rest; all of it; much of the time, by the seat-of-my-pants, learning as I ran. I figured it out the hard way, but thankfully, the camp grew. I was named the director after nine months.

Why did I survive all these years? Why would Jim, a friend of mine, with a business degree, experience with human resources, a former preacher, one who understood money, who could speak in public, last less than 2 years in his first camp director's position?

It is still a mystery to me; however, I firmly believe I was the right type of person for my position and Jim was the wrong type of person for his position. He had all the technical skills needed to run a camp; and I had very few. He had prior leadership opportunities at a church; I had none. He could speak eloquently; I could hardly lift my eyes from my notes when I first began making camp presentations. And currently, the camp where he was once the director continues to operate with the same number of beds and buildings as they did when he left 20 years ago. With the hand of the Lord on my head, directing and leading, my camp has grown by 800 beds and 70 buildings in 27 years. John Maxwell is right– "everything rises and falls on leadership."

But, I do believe there is more than just the director; I believe the board behind the director is the key factor, which allows the person to function according to their skill set and their personality traits. The board hired me, and they let me grow and develop and lead with what I had available IN me. They expected no more, and they did not try to redirect me. They did not insist I become a great public speaker. They didn't insist I be a high powered fund raiser. They let Earl be Earl and they let me run as hard and as fast as I could and they never put a bit in my mouth. I was able to work in my strengths.

In reality, the camp board and I were on parallel tracks; they set the policy and the general direction, while I went along side of them in the same direction, securing the railroad ties between the two rails– the board and myself. I developed the systems to make the camp grow. I wasn't that smart, I just worked hard. I had no training, but the board did not interfere with how I laid the ties between us. They were happy as long as we were moving and were both heading in the same direction— fulfilling the same mission: to bring salvation to the lost through Jesus Christ our Lord and to encourage and disciple believers in the faith.

Back to my friend Jim— it was simple. He never aligned himself to the direction of his board. His rail ran west, and the board's rail ran north: they wrecked and he left, leaving the camp wounded and crippled— still trying to recover 20 years later. They became stunted, stalled and stagnant– though a medium sized camp– there has been no additional growth in 20 years.

Yep, Maxwell was right, "everything rises and falls on leadership."

## *Points to Ponder*

1. Do we feel aligned to the direction of our board? What signs are there which verify our position with the board?

2. Do we sense we have clarity about the policies that our board has developed to which we should align ourselves?

3. What is my skill set?

4. What are my weaknesses?

5. Why do I believe I am the right fit for the job I now hold?

*"There are many different kinds of gifts, but the same Spirit."*

*2 Corinthians 12:4*

# CHAPTER 3
## Boards and Budgets

N**o two boards are made up the same. Some meet six times a year while others can handle all the business in four meetings. Some board members are elected for life while others serve a pre-determined term– in most cases three years. Some boards want to take part in work days while others see their service to the camp best served during their regular scheduled board meetings. Some boards want to manage the camp while many want to govern the camp.**

If you have a board made up of men and women who want to manage the operation– you have trouble. **Big trouble!** They become a bit in your mouth. They become a load on your back. They become shackles to your feet. They slow you up. They weigh you down. They trip you up with their second-guessing and micro-managing.

They mean well... or at least they think they do.

Some camp boards try to act like a church board: or should I say, some individual members want the board to act like a church board— making operating decisions such as approving the purchase of a copy machine. I sat on a church board, for one term— that was the business that filled most of our meetings— giving the pastor permission to do things. Nothing proceeded without permission. Camp boards that are stuck in this mode of operation are killing the camp— meeting by meeting. They are truly living out the book, *Death by Meeting*, by Patrick Lencioni.

It is the smaller, older camps that deal with this challenge the most. Their camp has evolved from a little summer camp operation run by volunteers, but managed by the board of directors who were forced into making every decision throughout a calendar year. In the early days, there were no budgets, only check book balances. There were no long range plans, only what do we do next summer? There were no strategic planning committees, there were workdays on Saturday— all board members were expected to attend. And for that time— it worked!

The camp grew and flourished and gradually moved from a volunteer work force to hiring a care-taker who had the oversight of grounds and development. Sometimes he handled the summer programs, sometime volunteers organized and managed the program.

The 80's came and suddenly a director was hired; someone to run the whole show— but the board was not told that— or at least the board did not change from their operational position. The fight was on. Strong, micro-managing boards either fought with a strong leader, or they were mollified into hiring a weak leader that they could control. Many potential "great" directors were sent packing due to a misunderstanding of who was in charge.

If you have not been at your camp long enough and not figured out which position your board is operating from by now, you will learn soon enough.

I believe I was hired to direct. I believe I was hired to lead. I believe I am empowered to make the decision of whether I buy the $600 copier, or the $999 color copier. I know how the camp functions best. Camp board members are wonderful people full of business and ministry ideas that are appropriate for their own careers and livelihood, but they don't know camp.

They don't understand the need to make a rush decision to buy a lift station pump on Friday morning when a group is already on the road to retreat in a building serviced by the pump. They don't know that I need to paint outside walls or inside rooms when I have extra staff or an unexpected opening in the retreat schedule that allows me to do so. They don't know that I have 14 Awana presentations in the next 7 weeks and I need a vehicle to get me there and back.

Here is what I want the board to know. I want them to approve a budget prior to the beginning of every year which lays out my spending opportunities. I declare: I hope to spend $4200 on office equipment— period. They don't need to know what size, what brand, what color. All they need to know is that I am planning to utilize $4200 to upgrade our office system the best way I know how. The list goes on— whether program supplies, maintenance needs, or kitchen equipment. I want to decide who, what, when, where and how. The camp board approves a budget that gives me guidelines to my year's purchasing.

Why would a board want to micro-manage the camp? **Lack of trust!** They don't trust who they have hired to do the job required to operate the facility and program to **THEIR** satisfaction or expectations. I have one question for this type of board- "What in the heck were you thinking when you hired this director? You have hired the wrong person if you can't trust them!"

Semantics matter: Controlling boards call the person in charge at camp the Manager. Empowering boards call them Executive Director. Controlling boards want their person to run **their** camp— **their** way. Empowering boards give Executive Directors freedom within the guidelines and policies set up by the board. Controlling boards make rules. Empowering boards make general policies. Controlling boards decide paint and carpet colors. Empowering boards allows directors to fix, repair, and remodel as the director sees fit and as he has time and money available.

Get the picture? You probably know which kind of board you are working for now.

Camp board members come and go, but usually the camp director is the constant thread in the management and oversight of the camp. Every three to six years, a board member leaves and a new one is appointed or elected by the governing body of the camp. It is a perfect system that ensures freshness, new perspective, and dictates turn over. Boards which never have elections or not in a rotating schedule create their own set of problems— usually called stagnation!

I don't personally get to pick the board members. The district of churches which owns the camp votes on the candidates. If I could create the *most-wanted features* to be found in a board member, the list would include the following: team player, problem solver, fun-minded, creative thinker, financially savvy, business-minded, ministry-focused, concerned parent, wise grandparent, budding theologian, and a friend. I don't want them to look alike, smell alike, think alike, or dream alike. I want farmers, mothers, bankers, truck drivers, lawyers, teachers, I.T. guys, accountants and preachers, each bringing their individual perspectives to the meetings.

How do I educate the influx of new board members who arrive fresh to their first board meeting, after serving faithfully on their own church board for years and years? I send the new board member a letter welcoming them to the board, by laying out the guidelines of what the board does and how it performs its duties. I tell the new board member to not interfere in the daily operations of the camp by INDIVIDUALLY seeking out staff members for input or to dig up dirt. I tell them that all opinions are welcome in the context of the board meeting and will be agreed upon as an ENTIRE board. I tell them our history as a board and bring them up to date on some recent decisions the board has made. I try to bring them up to speed about future development plans and financial positions of camp.

Once in a board meeting, I never ask their opinion about the color of paint; I ask the staff, because they know the camp best. I never ask the board to decide what type of chair to purchase; I bring them a picture and a price and tell them we bought this chair, for this reason.

When you start asking permission, you are inviting camp board members to revert back into becoming the small church board members. Don't start.

## *Points to Ponder*

1. From which position does my camp board operate? Hands on/permission granting or policy setting?

2. How do I need to adjust my thinking in order to adapt to this type of board?

3. How can I know that I am the right person to work with this board?

4. What can the board learn from this chapter?

5. How will I approach the next board meeting? Will I ask permission or forgiveness?

6. Do I feel trusted by the board? When have I not felt trusted by the board?

*Remind them to be submissive to
rulers and authorities, to be obedient,
to be ready for every good work.*

*Titus 3:1*

## CHAPTER 4

# Eight Reasons Why Some Camps are Stunted

**W**hy is the stunted camp suffering? Why can't the stunted camp gain traction? What are the underlying issues that have caused the "circling of the drain" effect to the stunted camps? If you are not circling the drain, perhaps you can at least see the drain from your position. Here is a list of eight reasons. Any one or combination of the eight can create havoc and lack of clarity, causing a camp to lose HOPE, and become stunted.

Remember, stunted means not growing into your full potential; it doesn't describe your size, it describes your condition.

**The possible reasons for a camp to become stunted are:**

1. There was a poor transition from a long-time director or founding director to their replacement. There was not a gradual transfer of the old culture and systems to the new director. The board did not

anticipate soon enough, or the old, long-time director was resistant to turning over any responsibility
while they were still in charge.

2. It is a fact— people die. Which means donors and
   volunteer workers die as well. Without the proper
   development of new and younger donors and volunteers, the camp gradually finds itself without enough
   money and no help. This problem is usually tied into
   one issue— the transfer of power from old to new.

3. The camp board maintains the role as the manager
   instead of as a governing body. The board continues
   to use the same board structure/job description/
   systems of the board from 40 years ago.

4. The camp board has hired the wrong **type** of new
   director: Most often a camp director is hired because of their theological and management training, and not their abilities to fix, repair and rebuild
   a facility. MOST MINISTRY FUNCTIONS OF THE
   CAMP ARE NOT BROKEN— IT IS THE FACILITY
   THAT IS BROKEN! Boards don't match the skill set
   with the needed job description.

5. No congruent master plan is in place as director after director comes and leaves, after only staying one
   to three years.

6. There is no business plan; the camp does not understand the bed principle which simply states: add
   more beds and you will increase your cash flow!
   Beds and plates equal revenue.

7. Many camps should not have become a year-a-round retreat facility in the first place. They are investing time and effort in trying to become a retreat facility— but maintaining horrible buildings, beds, and plates- which in turn cannot generate any momentum to regain traction. It is like trying to put on a ball (Cinderella-type ball), but holding it in a stable, with no orchestra (only a band called THE BAD BEDS), and handing out moldy bread and water for the main entrée. (Forgive my word picture)

8. Salary expenses are not in proportion to the rest of the budget. This is actually caused by many of the points listed above, but the circling of the drain is simply caused by not having enough income and having too much out-go. Dave Ramsey, the financial guru, tells it correctly on his radio talk show- "Lady, you need to make more money! And at the same time Lady, you need to stop spending money on everything you see on late night TV!"

**Here is a list of symptoms that manifest themselves when a camp is stunted:**

- No or little support from former donating churches or individuals

- Clutter-junk-broken furniture in many buildings

- Overall condition of the facilities is run down— routine maintenance has been deferred too long

- Rapid turnover of camp directors, each only lasting

one to three years— hiring too young and they lack skills and resolve

- The board has their back turned to the future, their face to their glory years, and they are determined they can resurrect the camp back to their glory years using the same procedures/conduct as they did forty years ago

- Can't get volunteer work crews out anymore

- Bad web site in which there is a tone in the script that screams three things: you're desperate, you're without hope or vision, and you're weary in bones and buildings

- Board members overreach their own board position and seek out staff to find out the real condition of camp, undermining the director

**Here are some possible solutions that would help to move a stunted camp into a mature camp.**

The items listed below are in the order that I deem most important to the least important.

**First:** You must reinvent the camp board. The board must stop being the board that gives permission to a director on every detail. Instead, the board must evolve quickly into a board that gives a director broad operating principles that they must implement in the operation of camp— a policy setting board. Examples could be:

- *Principle #1-* We will operate the camp with no debt.

- *Principle #2-* We will hire only born again, Spirit filled Christians to work for the organization.

- *Principle #3-* All new construction should be financed at least at the 50% level before the first shovel of dirt is turned.

Camp boards need to buck up and admit they are the cause of many of the camp's problems: instead of being Obama-like and say, "I was not informed... the state department decided", the board needs to be Truman-like and say, "The buck stops here." It is their role as the board to operate in a fashion that gives the camp director a chance to SUCCEED! Many boards are asking the director to lead, and build, and market- but they cut off his fingers, whack him in both knees and shackle him with layers and layers of red tape just to buy a hammer! That is the model for the government! The lean and the fast win. The slow and the clumsy lose.

Theodore Roosevelt said it this way, *"The best executive (board) is the one who has sense enough to pick good men to do what he wants done, and the self-restraint enough to keep from meddling with them while they do it."*

*This would be good advice for a board to follow!*

**Second:** The board needs to hire the right **TYPE** of director. Don't throw a person into a camp which needs remodeled, if they only want to lead Bible studies, run summer camp, counsel people, or preach. That is not the need! You need sweat equity. You need common sense. You need practical solutions to major building deficiencies. You need a family who can stay committed through the lean years.

You need someone who can cast a clear vision for the future— providing the guest groups hope that the ship can float again. You need a carpenter, not a theologian. You need a strong-willed person, not a weak-kneed mama's boy. You need a person with the heart of a nurse but with the resolve of a middle-line-backer. You need one who can prioritize and implement, not a dreamer of fantastic, rose-colored ideas who only takes their dreams as far as their lips—blah, blah, blah. You need someone whose life mantra is, "Yes I Can," not one who feebly voices, "I hope I can."

**Third:** You need someone who is willing to tackle the small stuff... *It is all small stuff:* de-junking; painting; planting flowers; cleaning buildings thoroughly; reinventing or re-arranging rooms to create new functions. You need to revitalize old buildings first- if you don't deal with the old first, you will be creating what I call: *The Ugly Sister Syndrome!* (More on this later.)

**Fourth:** You need to create a one year plan of what is to be accomplished. A three year plan of attack and then a five year plan of projects to be completed: being specific down to the last piece of tile or how many new light fixtures you are going to buy.

**Fifth:** You need to restore the donor's and guest's trust... in reality; this will happen if the first four points are dealt with quickly and with perseverance and resolve.

## *Points to Ponder*

1. What type of board is overseeing the camp?

2. How do I know I am the right type of person to accomplish the mission?

3. Do I enjoy doing the small stuff? What small stuff do I like doing? What small stuff do I dislike doing?

4. Do we have an actual plan that lays out the direction of the camp for the next five years? If not, what steps are needed to get one?

5. Have we lost the donor's and our guest's trust? What small victories can we accomplish in the next 30 days to shift the momentum to generate trust?

*But select capable men from all the people—*
*men who fear God, trustworthy men*
*who hate dishonest gain— and appoint them as*
*officials over thousands, hundreds, fifties and tens.*

*Exodus 18:21*

## CHAPTER 5
# Stunted— What does it Look Like?

When I consider the phrase "stunted camp," I visualize the miniature horse; all the parts are there- it has a mane and a tail, it has four legs and a head and his body connects all the parts: it is like this miniature horse stopped growing and maturing into a real horse- a horse that can be saddled and ridden or harnessed and driven. To the miniature horse I want to say, "Grow up, mature and make something out of yourself, besides being a hay burner!"

Stunted camps are caused by all types of reasons previously mentioned: boards, directors, proper leadership, money, old buildings, lack of vision, and perhaps even location. All the parts are there: pool, dining room, beds, plates, office building, cabins, boats, towers, swings, and staff— it looks like a horse, it smells like a horse, it feels like a horse- but it's just a horse caught in its own DNA– culture– and cannot grow and become a useful, full service animal.

What causes a miniature horse to remain a miniature horse? His DNA! His mother and father were miniatures, so he will be a miniature; he could not grow into a 15 hand horse if he wanted to.

The same is true with camps. Some are intentionally designed by the parents to remain small and intimate and only minister to a limited number or a certain population of people.

Our district owns one of these camps: Rock River is set up for 25 to 35 people. It was meant for a pastor to come away and study and have quiet; or a board retreat to plan, pray and prepare. Children are not allowed and quiet and restful is the atmosphere.

Hidden Acres, the other district camp is just the opposite: its DNA— given by the same parents as Rock River— allows us to grow and prosper with as many buildings as we can build. We have nearly unlimited grounds to develop and we have a growing church population caused by a rapid church planting program. We must be a 15 hands type of camp. We could grow into a draft horse if the Lord tarries. Same parents but different sizes, and completely different scopes. Each is a successful, vibrant, living organization because each is **living up to its full potential.**

The stunted camp is not necessarily small, medium or large: the stunted camp is stunted because it is not living up to its potential in regards to how it was designed and purposed. It is just the average little camp and it is the average large camp that plugs along- drifting backwards for a time, and then drifting a little forward. It exists, but it is not flourishing. It is the camp that could be here in five years, or it could be the camp that gets sunk by one catastrophe or even a few small bumps in the road; like the book of James says, "it is unstable in all its ways."

Stunted small camps struggle; stunted medium camps survive, and stunted large camps have reached a plateau, and are unable to move any further. Let me paint a picture of each size of camps.

**Small Camps-** Small camps which are stunted are in a panic mode. There is no vision. There is a lack of excitement. There is a lack of dollars. There is a high turn-over in directors. They exist from board meeting to board meeting, never knowing if the board could walk in and say, "It's all over, we might as well sell the place and put our energy somewhere else." Usually the stunted small camp is floundering in all areas: beds, plates, facilities and its small staff is overworked and underpaid.

**Medium Size Camps-** The medium size camps are the camps that are surviving by sheer hard work and determination from the staff of four to eight full time workers. There is not much momentum, and there are few victories to crow about. They have a loyal following of summer campers and retreat guests. They pay the bills, but one unexpected cancellation of a large retreat sets them back; there is no emergency contingency fund. This camp has a nice variety of program options. Sometimes ongoing maintenance is replaced by patches and paint— trying to make the facility look nice. There needs to be more revenue generated to support the structure and size of the camp, but as is, the staff is again overworked; there is never any floater staff available to fill holes.

**Large Camps-** This is the camp that should move on into an extra large camp. There is the constituency to support the camp, but the camp lacks the systems to grow the camp into something bigger and better. All the bells and whistles are in place that make this a great camp to attend. However, it functions a bit awkwardly internally- it needs to mature its systems to the current size and scope of its facility and staff. I would say the staff is contented and under-challenged in this camp. There is an attitude that pervades and says, "We have arrived at large," and everyone is extremely satisfied. To become a vibrant, growing organization would take everyone to step up in their individual duties: raising the bar in performance and attitudes. They are content with being some people's favorite, but not all the people's favorite.

I am never contented. I am not contented until the camp has become everyone's favorite. I don't want to be shoulder hugged; I want to be kissed on the lips!

I am not interested in the fact if I am ahead or behind another camp. I need to know that I am working as hard as I possibly am able to accomplish all that I possibly can, with the manpower and resources that are made available to me. If I am ten buildings ahead of the neighboring camp- who cares? If I have 50 less beds than another camp- who cares? I don't benchmark off of other camps; I benchmark off what I think could be possible at my camp.

My strength is going fast and straight and charging ahead; I must be content in my own skin.

Am I competitive? You bet. Do I want to be the best? Sure. Do I look at another camp and say, "We are better than that camp, we must have arrived?" Never! I am never content. I am momentarily satisfied, but not content.

Contentment can lead to rest— and rest could be taken over by sleep— and sleep lies next to death. I prefer to keep moving.

## *Points to Ponder*

1. Are we content with where we currently stand as a camp? Where do we stand today?

2. What signs are there which point to the fact that we are in a survival mode?

3. What will it take for the entire staff to understand what it will take to grow our camp to the next level?

4. Are there weak staff members who will not grow up into the next level? How are we going to build into the weaker staff members?

5. What steps can we take to ensure constant growth in systems and in services?


*Nevertheless, each one should
retain the place in life that the Lord assigned to him
and to which God has called him.*

*I Corinthians 7:17*


*(My interpretation— Grow where you are planted!)*

## CHAPTER 6
# Evolve or Dissolve

By December 1 of every year, I am ready to begin the year-end-reviews of every full time staff member and interns. For the first 20 years I didn't do it consistently. I did not like the process.

Something happened around year 20: I began to like the two hour session with each staff member. It has grown since then; staff is given questions to prepare for their meeting with me, instead of arriving cold-turkey for the interview. They come prepared. They know what they want to say and so we begin to talk. From the questions, many rabbit trails are chased down. We seldom stick exactly to the prepared script— but it gives both parties a place to start and finish.

I use this time to hear what they have liked doing over the past year and I hear what they have not enjoyed doing. I hear their personal goals and they tell me where they would like to grow and learn. My ears tune in to what I hear they are passionate about. I see with my eyes, as they discuss the things they do— just because it has been assigned to them— mundane tasks that must be done.

Discussions follow, we close in prayer, and they go back to work. I begin to mentally tweak their position.

We are a different camp every 12 months- each year a new building is built. Each year a new staff member is hired. Each year new programs are added. Each year old programs are eliminated. Each year we add more trucks, add another horse, or build another gaga pit. In one sense we are the same camp, we just operate differently from 12 months ago.

In many cases, work assignments and responsibilities get assigned to those who are either available or willing. Sometimes it is one, sometimes it is both. Not all assignments are a great fit, but it will get us by until we can take time to figure it out. I will adjust in the middle of the year if I have to, but I do most of the adjusting after our year-end-review time; December 10 to the 31st is change time.

As soon as the interviews are over, I start to evaluate and tweak.

The staff has gotten used to it. They almost make it a game as to what new or additional project or responsibility they will get assigned for the next year. I listen. I hear comments like, "I would love to have my own daycare," or, "It is not working well for me to work with this staff member on this project," or, "I would like to spend more time in the kitchen," or, "I would like to be able to do and learn all the special projects that Elly works on."

I move. I adjust responsibilities. I create new titles. I create new jobs. I reassign staff to new work. I take from one and give to another. I am trying to place everyone in the right seat on the bus. I am trying to find each person's sweet spot so that we can get 100% production knowing that they will be passionate about their work, if it is the right fit.

And next year, I will start again... moving, tweaking, reassigning, adjusting... because another year has come and gone, and we are not the same camp as we were 365 days before.

Every organization moves, changes, evolves with systems and styles and rhythms which must all gel together into a strong working unit. When you adjust every year, your internal systems keep pace with your physical growth.

Our churches have evolved; we now have drums and guitars– in place of the piano and organs. Farmers have changed; they now have electronically driven, $450,000 combines to cover the thousands of acres of row crop in the fraction of the time that their dads took to harvest. There used to be bookstores; now there is Amazon. There used to be record shops on the square; now we have I-tunes. There used to be landlines; now there are smart phones.

If you are not evolving, you are probably stunted. If you have not added a new building, a new staff, a new program– you are probably stunted. If you are the same shape as you were a year ago– then consider yourself stunted. There is nothing wrong with not changing– if you like the condition of irrelevance.

General Eric Shinseki said it best, *"If you don't like change, you're going to like irrelevance even less!"*

## *Points to Ponder*

1. Who is sitting in the wrong seat on our camp bus?

2. What new role or responsibility needs to be created to get this person sitting in the right seat?

3. If our camp has changed in size (either to the positive or negative), have I adjusted staffs' responsibilities to parallel to this size change?

4. What new staff needs to be added to our equation? Or, what staff position needs to be eliminated?

5. Can we as a staff begin to look at the year-end-reviews differently– not as a performance evaluation only– but as a time to adjust responsibilities to meet everyone's needs and interests?

6. How does the staff feel about the camp changing and evolving?

*I appeal to you therefore, brothers,*
*by the mercies of God, to present your bodies as a*
*living sacrifice, holy and acceptable to God,*
*which is your spiritual worship.*
*Do not be conformed to this world,*
*but **be transformed** by the renewal of your mind,*
*that by testing you may discern what is the*
*will of God, what is good and acceptable and perfect.*
*Romans 12:1-2*

## CHAPTER 7

# The Master's Plan

Y ou've seen them. They are filed away somewhere. Art Harrison, of Harrison Associates, could have been the designer of your camp master plan; perhaps it was done by some other architectural firm. They are exciting to look at and dream about. They help cast the original vision of the possibilities of the blank slate called raw ground. They generate excitement and give a visual description for donors to grab onto; it is a wonderful tool when casting the original vision.

I have one too. Art lives nearby and goes to one of our denomination's churches. He is my friend and he is knowledgeable in his field. But he is not a prophet or fortune teller; he is a visionary for **what could be at a camp**. In his mind's eye, he develops the best possible plan within the context and wishes of the founding camp board.

We have an air strip and a nine-hole golf course on ours. We have lakes. We have cabin areas. We have a radio station and a book store. We have outpost camps. We have lodges built across open fields located on the edge of a beautiful ravine. It all looks great on paper. It sells. It generates a response from a potential donor. It brings clarity to this vision called: our future camp.

Ten years out, the plan has been nearly lost in the filing cabinet. The 3-D model that was used as a visual aid sits on the top shelf in a storage building; reality sets in. Guest begin to arrive, usage demands another addition or a completely separate building with a completely different function. Never is the master plan consulted to decide where something gets placed according to Art. Remember, Art was imagining; it is your job to use common sense and place the building according to how your current guest groups are moving around the grounds. Art thought, you know.

I have been involved in every building built on our camp with the exception of the well house and where our staff house was moved onto the grounds and located. With the help of volunteers, I remodeled the staff house as my family lived in and around my dry wall dust. I helped plumb it. I helped wire it. I helped install new windows and doors. I helped build the garage and plant the 75 trees in its yard. I just didn't decide where it was to be placed. Thankfully, the board and house mover placed it where Art had told them.

The original lodge was placed where Art told us to put it also. Two out of 70 ain't too bad. It is not that we thought Art didn't know what he was doing– he did in fact. Art fore-saw the need for lodges, and cabin units, horse riding arena, and lakes. He saw open spaces, roads, and RV parks. He didn't miss a function. He was 100% accurate. He created the form— the ideal model— the picture on the puzzle box of pieces called a camp. The untrained director takes it from there.

The untrained director takes Art's professionally trained advice, glances at the general ideas and sets out to create or recreate an existing camp. Usually it will look like a twin, but not an identical twin.

We have no airport. We have no golf course. We have no book store or radio station. There was no need to build Art's ideas: the demand was not there. We have Amazon, and three Christian radio stations within 40 miles, and we were not willing to give up good Iowa farm ground to provide an airport for three or four of our original donors. Common sense takes precedence over the PLAN.

Some locations scream for a lodge with windows overlooking a view. Other hilltop ridges appear to be the spot that cabins should be strategically placed. The pond is placed where there is a good source of water and deep enough ravines to allow ample surface water. One building is added, then another, and pretty soon there is a full-fledged camp.

Older camps did not usually have the advantage of the services of an Art. Art came with a price tag that most founding directors would have found excessive; $20,000 would have built their first chapel/dining hall and several cabins in 1952. Volunteer labor– sweat equity– stretched the dollar. Recycled materials cheapened the building further.

In 1952, it made sense to place the chapel next to the road that entered the camp. "Why would we want to build another road when we already have one?" was the thought process of the founding site planner (board).

Today, camp directors are still living with the founding fathers reasoning, and to tell you the truth– it is a bit frustrating at times. Statements like, "If only they had put that building on the south fence line instead of the middle of camp," are heard everywhere I visit. It is called "builder's remorse."

If Art, the trained professional, could not see exactly into the future and imagine how patterns or program traffic demands would alter our camps, neither could your founding boards! So lighten up, when you talk and "wish" for something different at your camp. You have what you have, so use it now to the best of your ability.

I told you I have been around for the last 70 buildings! That is the secret to site development and planning. It is usually the camps who go through camp directors every three to five years who have a potpourri of camp buildings. A barn here, a lodge there, a recreation building stuck there. There is no congruent thought process as to the WHY a building should be placed in its particular location.

Each director has a particular taste in design or a particular location that is his favorite. Consequently, a building is built to suit his taste and placed where he THINKS would make a nice building location. Five directors in 20 years results in five different master plans.

And to make matters worse, the board members rotate on and off the board every three to six years, and seldom is there any of the original board members left to remember the whys of an original plan. You stick around for four or five years, if you are lucky you might get to build one or two buildings; if you stick around all your life you get to design, decide location, and build them all.

For those who are faithful or persistent and stick with a camp, they have the honor and the privilege to lay out the plan as he deems best. Ask Tom Robertson, from Fort Wilderness in Wisconsin. His dad, Truman, started the camp. Tom grew up at the camp. He heard his dad talk day after day about the barn or the dining room or about the tubing hill. He knew and lived the development of the camp; it is easy for him to know where the Gathering Place was to be built. He heard his dad say it in 1964 when Tom was 14 years old. Tom knows that the BBQ pit must stay in the center of the camp— outdoor cooking is at the center of the program that his father originally developed.

There is no pixie dust that one can sprinkle over an older camp to make all the buildings function well together— you just have to make the best of it, using your creative juices to reconfigure the insides into something that works for you in the here-and-now.

I have used a master plan; but it is called the *Master's* plan instead of Art's.

## *Points to Ponder*

1. Do we have a master plan? Where is it? And, have we followed it?

2. What older buildings are creating a challenge for us today?

3. What are we going to do to reinvent this building, so that it will be functional for today's guests?

4. Where will we place the next three new buildings? What is our time line to finish these projects?

5. How can we best combine the new and the old to function and flow together creating a group of buildings that work together instead of against each other?

*So we rebuilt the wall*
*till all of it reached half its height,*
*for the people worked with all their hearts.*
*Nehemiah 4:6*

## Chapter 8

# Never Give Up!

If you are reading this book, and your camp was built after World War II, but before 1959, I think I can describe you. Let me review your history. The first twenty years were fabulous. Every year something new was added. For many of you, the vision of camp was eclectically created: a cabin was built by the men's group of the Oak Grove church; the next year, another group of men from the Bangor Church became excited and they too brought their work crews to build their cabin.

For some, individual summer cabins resembled the first cabin built— following a similar floor plan and layout of beds. For others, it was a contest to see who could outdo the last group by adding a different feature. You are now the director of what I call a tossed salad camp- full of lots of good stuff and colors- but nothing complementing each other or even co-existing with any coordination of colors, design or building materials; you are eclectic!

If you are lucky, many of the first cabins have been drug off to distant points in need of a storage building for outpost camps or program storage. Their unique design is isolated or hidden from the rest of the camp, only providing shelter to a few guests who utilize the area. However, for many of you, there are still those original buildings, built with the sweat and power of faithful men, which are now sitting in the most prime real estate on the entire camp property. History and long memories begin to work against you.

Not only do you have a tired, non-functional building gracing the center of camp, you also have daughters of the founding men still alive reminding you of the fact, "my dad labored for 45 straight days to construct this building; no one will remove the memory of my father!"

You know the lady– she sits in front of you at church; probably named Millie. Millie is the sweet little casserole-toting lady who sits in her pew every week, every meeting, who smiles gently and asks you weekly how things are at the camp. This Millie is the same one who can corner the camp board member or staff member when even the slightest rumor that something was going to change at "her dad's camp." The friendly, gentle Millie turns into the face and voice that can turn back charging, hungry bears. Millie doesn't speak often, but when she does, she carries a very loud voice— people listen and the camp suffers.

Now you are stuck. You're a 31-year-old camp director, loaded with fresh innovative ideas, and have just taken over the reins of leadership of this ship. Nobody told you prior to signing on that you would have a 75-year-old, silver-haired grandma named Millie still at the rudder of your ship with her strong memory and emotions. Your hands feel tied and you begin to lose the hope and excitement for this ministry.

You might have even grown up in this camp and have loads of your own warm and fuzzy experiences that propelled you to take this position in the first place.

I do know your conditions. I do know what your buildings look like. I can see years of history and memories stacked into every corner of every building. I can guess your camp's age by your appearance; you are working at a place founded after World War II. As the soldiers returned home, there was enormous energy and drive to build a bigger and better America. Out of the 840 CCCA camps, many were founded during the decade following the war. Those were glory years; the same attitude that conquered Nazism, Fascism, and Japan, was now ready to tackle all of life back in America.

Churches began to understand the value of a camping experience. Former soldiers, who had returned to their farms, were more than willing to pitch in and create something called the Bible Camp. The men used their same farm-like intuition and abilities to build the first building on land that was usually donated by a well-intentioned church member; usually the rougher ground located near a lake or river.

Camps were erected without concern for population trends, nearby services, or even major highways. Interstates were not ready to tie together this great country. Camps were put in places near Deep River or Hastings or Ralston—mere villages at best, stuck in between corn fields and river bottoms. These villages could not help sustain the operation of the camp; they could only be great cheerleaders and occasionally give a helping hand to the little Bible camp outside of town.

I have two friends, sisters, whose father was such a visionary. He found a piece of land, and with sheer determination and drive, constructed his first camp building out of re-cycled red cinder block. He used rails discarded by the railroad as trusses and support beams for the two story building. The upstairs served as the chapel and the basement was the dining room. The rest of the camp was slower to develop, knowing that families and children could live in extremely primitive conditions until a solid cabin or a meeting space could be built.

Piece by piece, buildings were put in place; there was little thought or concern about guest group conveniences or personal care for the campers. Buildings landed in the spot that made the most sense to the farm-ingrained entrepreneur: under a shade tree or on the single most flat spot available. All this was done without much concern about how traffic would flow, how infrastructure would function, how guests would get from one building to the next. It worked: people were just happy to have their first primitive buildings up and in place, allowing them protection from storms and rain. The summer camp was boarded up when school began.

Did I just describe your setting? Have some of your buildings morphed from chapels, to dining halls, to dorm rooms, to now just storage buildings? Does your building's layout remind you of two or three jig saw puzzles thrown into one box for you to figure out? Do your buildings have additions which have further additions, with hallways and closets that start and end at unusual places? If you are answering yes, yes, yes, then keep reading.

There have been many, many good years of ministry in your camp, but just lately, you have gotten behind. You can blame the economy, you can blame Bush, you can blame your board, and you can probably blame Obama. At this point, you have a stunted camp on your hands and you wonder if there is any possible way to push ahead.

Winston Churchill said it so well when faced with the possibility of annihilation by the constant bombardment over England by the Germany Luftwaffe. The cities lay in shambles, families' nerves were on end from constant siren raids interrupting meals, sleep and work. When there was little hope of any victory, Churchill spoke directly to a group of students, and said, *"Never, ever, ever, ever, ever, ever, ever, give up. Never give up. Never give up. Never give up."*

I say the same.

Resolve is a wonderful character trait- most of our lives we are called stubborn, but once tragedy or a challenge develops, people around us call it "Resolve— Fortitude— Perseverance." I really don't care what you call it; I know that I am flat-out mule-stubborn with a streak of iron down my back. I will not be moved!

Can I be blunt with you? If you don't have this character trait- turn in your resignation, lock the door, and go find another job. It is all over. If this is your current predicament and you don't believe you have the resolve to face the dear Millies of your life- you are done. The Marines know it... they only want the GOOD men... not the weak ones. If Millie scares you, start looking in the want ads for a new job.

Apparently, you have decided you are stubborn too; you have continued to read. Good for you. You have decided that you are committed.

I love the Mel Gibson pose in the movie *Brave Heart*— face painted up, sword and shield in hand, leading the charge. I am no Mel Gibson; I am over weight, graying and a gentle grandpa on the outside; but on the inside I still have that Gibson-like demeanor that charges at the enemy. I still move towards the barking dog.

You are all dressed up like Gibson, you have the resolve of Churchill, but at this point you may not have identified the enemy. If you are new to camp ministry, there are more fog-like days than sunshine days; you are reeling from the lack of understanding of why and how your camp got stunted.

History is probably your enemy. Buildings are probably your enemy. Sewer lines are probably your enemy. Long-standing board members may look like the enemy. Location can be the enemy. Lack of program options is an enemy. Worn out mattresses have enemy-like tendencies complete with bed bugs. Your kitchen appears to be an enemy complete with belching ovens and temperamental walk-in freezers. No wonder you feel the fog of identifying your enemy; there are so many and they all are attacking you from every side.

Sit down and take a deep breath; remind yourself what drew you to the job in the first place. Remember your fifth grade counselor and how he walked with you down to the lake on that first Tuesday and asked you some personal questions about if you died, would you end up in heaven or hell? Do you remember your answer? Sure you do... it was during that week you probably gave your life to Christ. And the next year you came back and rededicated your life, and the next, and the next.

Finally, you became of age– you became a counselor and you were the one pulling the camper aside on Tuesday on your walk to the lake– you were the counselor who ended up leading the entire cabin of overly-rambunctious, rebellious Jr. High boys to Christ on Thursday night after the campfire— as you lay in the cabin and discussed eternal issues. If you can remember all this, your resolve should have become even stronger, and your iron will should be unbreakable.

Now go bake Millie a cake and go visit her. Tell her of your vision for the camp! She just might write you a check!

## *Points to Ponder*

1. Who are our "Millies" and where do they live?

2. Are we treating our history as an enemy or a foe?

3. What five things can we do with some of our older buildings to bring new life to them?

4. What groups of volunteers are best suited to help us win these victories?

5. What kind of cake are we baking for the Millies in our lives?


*What, then, shall we say in response to these things?*
*If God is for us, who can be against us?*

*Romans 8:31*

## Chapter 9
# Favorite Camp Status

**W**hat have we learned so far in the first eight chapters of this book? We understand that any size camp can become stunted for several reasons, but it usually is caused by a dysfunctional board- director relationship which is the result of a board hiring the wrong type of director who did not match well with the objectives and goals set by the board.

Once friction begins between a board and a director it could take outside intervention to correct the problem. Both parties are frustrated with each other and this will spill out onto the staff and also back to the supporting churches. If there is no resolution, unmet expectations become aggravation, and then aggravation becomes irritations, and finally irritation develops into dissension and strife. Strife can cause all movement of an organization to grind to a halt; it becomes stunted and stale: the camp is not dead, but the pulse is weak, and the slightest mishap can send the camp swirling around the drain.

Much of this book contains scenarios or stories of how I have overcome the small and new camp. How our camp has gained momentum. How our camp has developed a "trust" account with the board and our constituency. Have I made mistakes? Yes, and by the bucket loads. Have I had road blocks and blow ups? Yes, occasionally. Have we overcome the roadblocks? Emphatically yes.

Much of what I do at camp is solving problems. Unsolved problems create lack of clarity. Lack of clarity causes staff to doubt and grumble. Grumbling staff changes the culture of camp. An unstable culture is lived out in front of campers and retreat guests; it doesn't take long for everyone to pull back on trusting the camp to do a great job. Gradually you move from being their "favorite camp" to just being the "camp." One word changes everything: "favorite!"

What a simple concept; but what a powerful reality it is: *being someone's favorite camp*. Today, there is no shortage of things that can be the favorite in people's lives. The secret is tapping into their favor and staying in their favor for their entire lifetime.

There are many issues and responsibilities that come into play in finding favor in the lives of our guests. There are the facilities, the variety of programs, the registration process, the staff, the summer counselors, the condition of the grounds, the quality of the food, and the comfort of the beds.

Not once in this list is the size of a camp mentioned: it is the internal components. It is the many layers of how a camp functions and displays itself that creates favor and trust, which can generate a statement like, "this is my favorite camp."

We all want to be the favorite uncle: the fun one, the generous one, the happy one, the loving and caring one, the one whose house is always open and available with great food, and activities, and fellowship. I trust as you read the rest of the book, that you catch the vision of how you too can regain your favor, regain your vision, and become a revitalized organization regardless of size or scope: you will become a camp that is everyone's "favorite camp!"

## *Points to Ponder*

1.  How is our camp being talked about back home in the local churches?

2. What have we done right to deserve this coveted position in people's hearts?

3. If we are not being talked about as a favorite, what are we not doing correctly?

4. What simple things can we do to change how people perceive us?

5. How can we regain guest groups' and campers' trust– giving us a second chance to become their favorite camp?

*May God give you dew from heaven.*
*May He give you the richness of the earth.*
*May He give you plenty of grain and fresh wine.*
*May nations serve you.*
*May they bow down to you.*

*Rule over your brothers.*
*May the sons of your mother bow down to you.*
*May those who call down curses on you be cursed.*
*And may those who bless you be blessed."*

*Genesis 27:28-29*

## CHAPTER 10
# It's NOT Just the Boards!

Stunted camps become stunted for several reasons. We have discussed issues like the board who micro manages. We have discussed the wrong hiring of the wrong type of leader to run a camp. We have discussed boards nailed together many years ago in the wrong place— they are called your buildings. But that is not all that can hold a camp back; it is not all that will stunt a camp into a sub-par condition.

The next element that needs to be addressed in a stunted camp is its systems. It is the "how we do things" around camp! It is the director who dictates, "It is my way... or the highway." It is one part personality, mixed with two parts of business know-how, and throw in the amount of time and resources available: you have systems.

Systems are driven by the personality of the leadership. In most cases, even over-bearing boards do not get this deep into the operation of the camp. It is up to the director to mandate, implement, and execute his systems.

I have mine; they are called "Earl's way." Staff have come and gone from our camp and many times, as they are driving out the driveway for the last time, you can hear them say, "I could not accept the way Earl ran the camp." Translation: "I can't accept Earl's systems!" Notice, he wasn't saying he didn't like me, or that he thought I was wrong; he just could not adjust his mind to do the work of camp my way.

Let me give you an example. I hired a man to be our operations manager a few years ago. He was a great person; he had a nice family. But we just could not work well together. I would say "paint with green paint," he would paint with blue/green paint. I would say, "Mow the grass on Thursdays, so that it would look nice for parents on Fridays,"— he would mow on Tuesdays. His work was good; he just didn't accept my systems.

We cut firewood for our family campers; lots of firewood that we throw onto a big pile. It is centrally located in camp on a slab of cement. Note the words "throw onto a pile." The reason for the system of throwing– it takes less time and is more efficient than after splitting the wood, walking over and placing a stick of wood onto a neat stack. We don't charge for the firewood— family campers haul it out of there by the truck loads to their camp sites; I wanted to split and process the wood just as fast as I could: I wanted high production. Our former operations manager thought differently and fought me.

He was released from camp on a Thursday; as I drove into camp Friday morning the sun just happened to be shining on a newly, neatly split and stacked row of firewood. All I could say to myself as I saw the stacked wood, "And that is the reason you are no longer working for us!"

I tell you this story not to show to you that I am stubborn, dictatorial, or demanding: I am telling you because a system is in place for more than just a whim or personal leaning. It is in place so that ALL staff can understand: a system lays out how the business is run.

Many camps are stunted because there are too many people developing their own personal systems. Let me give you an example of such a camp that I recently heard about. Here are several systems which individual staff members enforce— as the system of their camp:

- We don't let guests walk on the grass because they will take "the just mowed" look from it.

- We don't want our guests to walk on the pathways when it is muddy, they will track mud into the buildings.

- We don't book retreats in December because we want to clean the carpets during that time.

- We will not accept any reservations over holidays so that we, the staff, can be gone.

- We only serve meals at 8-12-6; be here and be early. We will not move meal times to accommodate the guests.

When I heard this, I went straight through the roof. My first thought was, "I believe the staff is running the camp instead of the director." Just so you know, directors develop unified systems, and it's the staff's job to implement the systems; this is an important principle to understand if you are not the director. This is what a director is hired to do: direct the camp's systems!

For the next several chapters I will write about some of the systems that I have used. To several of my systems, you will say, "that won't work in our camp"- and I agree. Every camp must develop a cohesive culture of systems that are easy to understand, easy for all to implement, and easy to pass on and teach to new staff members. All camps currently have systems; the question would be: are they unified and come from the director, or are they a hodge-podge of personal demands that staff invent to make their jobs easier.

Much of the systems a director puts in place affect the over-all culture of the camp. There are tightly managed camps full of rules. There are the casual feeling camps that have just a minimal amount of rules. There is the frugal camp. There is the generous camp. There is the proud, cocky camp. There is the humble camp. Each has a specific flavor that is very evident to guests groups and staff.

None of the systems are more right or more wrong; what is− is. It is the job of the director to set the tone and provide the systems where all staff can do their job seamlessly, without friction, and with unified vision of the mission of the camp. When this is not in place− a camp can easily become stunted simply because proper systems are not in place so the staff can manage the amount of business the facilities could actually handle.

It is not enough to have systems in place. The systems have to translate into outrageously good service, wonderful friendly hospitality, generous amounts of high quality food, impeccable grounds, clean rooms, more than adequate meeting spaces with modernized audiovisual equipment, safe and friendly programs, spotless bathrooms, a registration process that is easy and accessible to ALL guests, and a staff that live out the life of a servant. Systems that don't allow staff to live out the above list are not positive systems; they are systems that will halt growth and ministry opportunities. They will cause the camp to become stunted!

I hope you enjoy reading the next few chapters. If for no other reason, you might think, "I could never work for him" and you might appreciate your own director more! Regardless, grow your systems in such a way as to meet your size and scope of your ministry with love and care; misaligned systems not only stunt you, if left un-clarified— they can kill you.

## *Points to Ponder*

1. What is the director's "way of doing camp?"

2. Does everyone buy into the director's ways?

3. What are the symptoms that are evident when an individual staff member resists the set of pre-described systems?

4. Has the director ever told the staff, "This is who we are and this is how we do things at our camp?"

5. Do you have someone on staff that is still stacking wood, when they should be throwing it? How will you deal with him?

*There is a way that seems right to a person, but eventually it ends in death. (Firing)*

*Proverbs 14:12*

## CHAPTER 11

# On My Knees: The Toilet Principle

**W**hen you first arrived at camp to serve, you were thinking the camping ministry was going to be a constant cycle of camp fires, singing, "Kumbayah my Lord," Bible studies, and winning young people to the Lord; but now you have found yourself down on your knees– in front of a toilet with a squirt bottle in one hand and a toilet brush in the other; this is definitely more than you imagined.

Get used to it. **95% of camp work is toilet cleaning.**

Not actually TOILET CLEANING, but like toilet-cleaning: serving, hidden away from most guests' eyes, creating a more comfortable, cleaner, tidier, prettier place in which the guests can enjoy and have their "encounter" with the Almighty.

During their first months, I have always tried to assign the new staff with a rabbit trail job that was not on their original job description. It would be something they would not usually volunteer for like: cleaning out the maintenance storage building; straightening out the back room of the office; unloading 186 sheets of 4' x 12' dry wall: the dirty and the grimy work; the stuff that nobody else wants to do.

Am I a sadist? Hardly! I want to see if they will be willing to put themselves into doing the mundane and filthy jobs with a servant's heart. I find out what they are made of and they find out if they are made for working at camp. Some are happy; and some are very unhappy.

I would never give a new staff member the responsibility of leading Bible studies and training young staff for summer camp ministry, if I can't see a happy heart that is willing to clean a toilet-like job. Do all things as unto the Lord, and do them with a smile and with gladness.

## *Points to Ponder*

1. What is my attitude when I am asked to do jobs that are below my training?

2. What am I learning while I am "on my knees?"

3. Do I know that even these jobs add value to the camp and the guests' experience?

4. Do I understand that these types of jobs are the training ground for greater things?

5. Where can I sign up for an "on your knees" experience that will help align my will to His desires?

*Whenever we do work
we should do that work
as if unto the Lord,
not as if we were working for man.
For doing so we'll be given
an inheritance from the Lord.*

*Colossians 3:23*

## CHAPTER 12

# It is a Pleasure to Serve You!

I love the Ritz-Carlton hotel. I have never personally been to one, but I imagine I would love to stay there. I love Ritz-Carlton because they get it— they exude hospitality. They know why they exist. Just ask any employee, from maid to front desk manager and they will all say, "We are ladies and gentleman, serving ladies and gentleman." I get that, and I am a man.

I get that because I understand what a lady and a gentleman should act like. And I certainly get what the Biblical interpretation of the word "serve" means; Ritz-Carlton's staff knows what the guest service industry is all about— intentional, hospitable service. Just tell a Ritz-Carlton maid thank you and she will always reply, "It is a pleasure to serve you!"

Ritz-Carlton— camp? What is the connection? People are people: rich people; poor people; country people; urban people; junior high people; senior saint people: all the same. God made them all— created them all alike, but with different finger prints and DNA. You must know that ALL people **crave love, affection and care**. Danny Meyers boils it down well in his book, *Setting the Table,* "We arrive as new babies and the first thing we get is eye contact, a smile, a hug, and food." Pretty basic stuff! Guess what? We don't really change much over the years— we are in need of attention (eye contact), acceptance (a smile), love (hug) and food! I am 59 and I am still needing each of these four basic needs.

If you're new to camping and you want your first retreat encounters to be a winner— then get with it and buy into the Ritz-Carlton mind set, "It is a pleasure to serve you!"

Adapt your systems to meet the guests' needs. Let me explain: Almost all of our registration processes are done online— mothers love being able to sit at their desk at work or home and get their kids or family registered for camp; it is easy and convenient for the ladies. Not so for the men: men want to call in and say, "I'll be there, write me down, and I am bringing 20 guys with me, and here is my credit card number!"

At first, our office staff resisted. They said, "We were told we needed to have a paper registration or the men must register online." I said, "Then change your system, because men will not do that... not now... not in the future... it just will not work!" Red Green spoke very honestly and correctly when he adopted the following mantra for his men's club, "I am a man, I can change, if I have to, I guess."

Judy, our office manager, gladly changed the system, and we now take phone reservations for both of our men's retreats. Does it infringe upon the time of the office staff? It sure does. It means more data entry by them. It means trying to keep all notes and scribbles straight. It means that our men guests are happy. It truly is a "pleasure to serve you!"

I recently tried to register for the CCCA sectional in Texas; being 59, I am not too smart on the computer. I made 25 attempts to get into their computer registration system. I was using the wrong portal! I finally emailed explaining my dilemma– Melissa said, "No, problem, I will get your name and information down– what is your T-shirt size?" Melissa gets it– she was more than willing to bypass the system to make sure I could get registered. I caused her more work. I caused her more paperwork, but Melissa saw this as an opportunity to serve me... with pleasure.

We talk up the three S's at our weekly staff meetings: to Serve, Solve and Sell. At least once a month, we remind the young staff members prior to a retreat to remember the three S's as they approach the weekend. Here is what we want each staff to have imprinted into their DNA of operation for the weekend:

**Serve:** We are here to serve you; we are here to make your weekend as unencumbered as possible. We don't want the guests to have to worry about sound equipment, beds, food, or whether or not the gym is opened. If they want to eat at 6:30 in the morning– we are ready with early morning smiles at 6:20. If they want to have their lunch down by the lake at noon– we have the picnic set up by 11:50. If they want to have an outdoor movie at 11:30 on a Saturday night– the theatre is open and we will even supply the popcorn– no charge! We never say "We can't do that!" Our mantra is, "Yes, we can!" We never let "the rules of camp" interfere with our ability to serve our guests.

**Solve:** If you have a problem, we are here to solve it. As a matter of fact each staff member knows that when a problem is presented to them by a guest, that they "own the problem"– it is that particular staff person's responsibility to ensure that the problem is solved. Does that mean the cook needs to drop what she is doing to go fix the hot water heater in a building? No, but she is the one to relay the information to the maintenance staff, who in turn does the actual fixing. However, it is the job of the cook to check back with the maintenance man to see if the job is completed. It is the cook's job to find the guest and report to him-your problem is solved! This is not an issue that will wait until next Tuesday to be resolved: this is an A.S.A.P. issue that needs immediate attention; all staff members are empowered to make it happen– NOW!

What does this tell our guests when we solve their roadblocks? They feel cared for! Do you want a guest to return home and become your biggest cheerleader? Then care for them. Do you want this retreating mother to send her kids back to summer camp? Then care for her in January at ladies' retreat and you will build up your summer camp numbers. Do you want the man who you helped register for men's retreat to send you a year-end check in December? Then care for him in March at the Sportsman's retreat.

**Sell:** We want every staff person to sell. Canteen stuff? No— sell our camp. Sell the next event. Sell summer camp. Sell the next project. Sell opportunities to give towards a project. Sell the vision of the camp. Sell the mission of the camp. Sell is actually the word promote. We want every staff member to know so much about everything that even the dishwasher is current about what is ahead on the schedule, what the next project is going to be, and to understand how summer camps work. I never want to hear a staff person say, "I don't know," without also saying, "but let's find out."

I can see your mind spinning. I can hear your next question, "How does this apply to the little camp just getting by? Ours is just ma and me here at the camp– we don't have time for all this soft stuff!" *Did you ever think that the reason you might just be getting by is because of how you are actually treating your guests?* Did you ever evaluate your systems to see if they truly are "user friendly?" Or have you just settled into a routine that works best for you– the director?

If you can adjust your way of thinking, you can revolutionize the culture of your camp. Without spending a dime on boards, or paint, or new carpet to revitalize the buildings, you can adjust how guest groups are treated– and eventually adjust how guest groups perceive you as their camp.

My wife and I raised our kids on *Psalty—The Singing Song Book*. Do you remember that? The one song that has stuck in my head after 25 years is: "If you want to be great in God's kingdom, you must be a servant of all." I will paraphrase it in camp lingo: If you want to be a great camp, offer great customer care— full of actions which show, "we care for you!"

Good camps are stalled and stunted because they don't "get it;" they don't get that if you treat the guests and campers with warmth and affection, they will beat a path back to your doorstep next year, to get more love and care smothered on them. Remember our first encounter in our life—our mothers looked us in the eye, we received a smile, we were hugged, and we took in great food— now go, and do like-wise with your guests.

## Points to Ponder

1. What systems do we have in place that create roadblocks for our guests to be successful?

2. What five procedures can we adjust this week to make our guest groups feel cared for?

3. Who on staff is to be assigned the "hospitality" queen position?

4. Are we acting as the guest groups' agent or are we acting more like a gatekeeper– making sure everyone does their retreat our way? How can we become a retreat's agent?

5. How do the entire staff know that they are empowered to solve guests' problems?

6. Are we stunted and stalled because we have not made a careful analysis of our ways of doing camp? How would we rate our camp? Are we claiming to be an A- camp when in reality we are a C+ camp at best?

*It shall not be so among you.*
*But whoever would be great among you*
*must be your servant.*

*Matthew 20:26*

## CHAPTER 13

# I Don't Like Fund Raising Either!

**I** don't like to fund raise! There, I said it. It is heresy amongst big camp people. Seminars are led by high powered fund raisers who insist that every camp director should be on the road, drinking coffee with donors, planning banquets, tooting the camp's horn and asking directly for money for their next capital campaign, their next building, their next dream.

I have attended countless fund-raising seminars over the years in sectional and national conferences in hopes that I could muster up the skills and passion to hit the road. They all said the same thing, "If you don't ask for the money, you are cheating people out of their Biblical responsibility." I felt guilty; I felt ashamed; I just couldn't do it.

I have really tried to do it their way.... but I have failed. I did try to take an elderly lady out for lunch— once. I felt like a pig on a racetrack— awkward and I stunk. That was 24 years ago: never again.

So instead of traveling and interacting with donors in a one-to-one format, I did what I do best; I did things. When it was time to raise a million dollars to match a million dollar gift for our Family Life Center, I walked 350 miles across Iowa in 22 straight days; it was a gimmick rather than a strategy. When it came time to build the Inn, I needed a way to draw attention that we needed to add beds; so I slept in an army tent during the entire month of June for 30 straight nights. I survived intense summer storms, the death and burial of my father, and more mosquitoes than I care to mention— the bed was hard and the nights were full of Iowa humidity. It didn't feel like fund raising: it felt natural, it felt fun; it brought awareness to the project— and the people gave... generously.

When asked how I raise money, I always say, "Well, I am not very good at actually raising money, but when I do raise money, I do it the old fashion way... I earn it." I earn it by building and protecting the trust of the people. I earn it by building buildings when and how I say I am going to build them: on budget and on time. I keep the projects well defined and simple. I state a purpose and plan. I rely on the speed and power of trust.

Stephen M.R. Covey writes in his book, *The Speed of Trust*, "trust allows for increased speed at a lower cost." People like the vision we present, and they give. We present a purpose and a plan and they buy into it and respond. I have no idea where the next check will come from. I never worry; I have seen His faithfulness time and time again. I can rest on that. Seldom is all the money in hand before we begin digging— we keep ordering from the lumber yard and the bills always get paid.

Plus, this type of fundraising frees me up to stay close to home and mind the business— the knitting— the operation.

I become the driver of the projects– not the builder, but the driver. We have a full time builder. He pays attention to levelness issues. He worries about structural integrity. He makes sure the walls are straight and the ceiling is packed with insulation at an R-45 level. I drive the project. Seth, our builder, is our brains; I am the push. I keep all people busy, all people focused and all people engaged, both volunteer and paid staff.

So it is okay with me if you stay home. If you are in a small camp, there is plenty to do. You don't have to be away on the road meeting and greeting. I think it is wonderful for those who do it faithfully– it works perfectly for their system and for their donors.

However, you can relax and know it is okay just to keep your head down and plow away at the work at home. Donors will pay attention. Donors know progress. Donors hear good reports through the church grapevine. Donors see changed lives and hear fourth graders give testimonies in church. Donors are smart people who have worked hard to accumulate a savings account; they want to trust those to whom they give it. Trust me, you ARE fund raising– it just doesn't feel uncomfortable or awkward.

To this day, I can't even take up an offering; I never want to leave the impression that I am taking something– I want our people to give it– freely– and they do!

Seventy new buildings: $0.00 interest paid out; $0.00 debt balance. Isn't God good? Doesn't He like to surprise those who toil under the sun from morning until night?

You can take this advice to the bank, Jack!

## *Points to Ponder*

1. What is our philosophy about raising money?

2. What plan will we utilize to raise money for a capital campaign?

3. How does the "mind the knitting" approach work in my camp?

4. What projects have we promised in the past, but were unable to deliver the goods to the donor?

5. What project are we currently working on that has no "driver?"

*"As for every man to whom God has given
riches and wealth,
and given him power to eat of it,
to receive his heritage and rejoice in his labor—
this is the gift of God."*

*Ecclesiastes 5:19*

## CHAPTER 14
# Listen to Your Critics...

*"You can please some of the people some of the time,
all of the people some of the time,
some of the people all of the time,
but you can never please
all of the people all of the time."*

Abraham Lincoln

Dear old Abe said it best– not everybody is going to like you or what you do or how you do it. There is just a certain group of people who will complain that your ice cream is too cold, too soft, too sugary; your beds are too soft, too hard, too high; that your food is too brown, too yellow, too green; your lawn is too dry, too short, too long; your pool is too wet, too cold, too warm; your zip-line is too high, too fast, too slow. You know the type I am sure! Every group has at least one or two like this; you learn to deal with them by smiling through your clenched teeth.

But there are those who truly do care and take the time and energy to write the camp a note or tell a staff person who is on duty for the weekend; those are the ones you want to re-spond to immediately. Unresolved guest issues become trip-ping points. Guests remember the little issues that tripped them up over the weekend, longer than they remember what a wonderful weekend they just had at your camp.

I believe that most of these "complaints" or "issues" would be minimized if there was a more stark transition from sum-mer camp to the retreat schedule. It took us years before this principle finally sunk in: summer camps run this way, and retreats run that way. Let's look at why guests "complain."

I know your schedule: six or eight or even 10 weeks of sum-mer camp. Around August 1, the counselors head home and the retreat groups begin to arrive. All staff is preoccupied and exhausted from the summer, so the retreat business slips up on everyone: the buildings are not quite as clean as they should be; there is left-over summer camp food in the freezer that needs to be used up; there is lost and found clutter scattered in every camp building. Summer camp wears on a camp facility. The summer camper is messy, dirty, and sometimes a bit smelly.

The guest groups begin to arrive and immediately feel like they are summer campers in adult bodies: the buildings have a very "used" feeling and look about them; the menu of tacos, or chicken strips, or hot dogs is not what their stom-achs had anticipated; they are herded into lines that resem-ble a pre-school outing– stand in line please and wait.

No wonder there are complaints. I hate dirty. I hate school lunch food. I hate standing in line longer than a minute.

Camps actually set themselves up for the barrage of complaints when they attach the words Conference Center to their name. Camps are no longer the Bible camp for kids; camps have morphed into a Conference Center. And in the guest groups' minds, that speaks something quite different than summer camp.

Your guests attend other conferences with their work; they might attend the Four Seasons Hotel– they are used to a certain look, a certain feel, a certain level of service and hospitality. When they arrive at your camp and conference center, and you provide a bed with a three inch mattress, feed them a plate full of yellow- chicken strips, mac' 'n' cheese, and fruit cocktail— they have a legitimate reason to write you a critical note. You didn't perform up to your name. You are not a conference center— you are a summer camp with adult guests.

The flip from the end of summer camp into the retreat season is the quickest and most drastic of our five yearly transitions. Often we have less than 24 hours to make the change: because of that, we have to give extra thought and care into this transition. We will assign at least one person to see that the transition happens well. We either hire extra housekeepers, or we move extra summer staff into the "transition team."

Regardless of how small or how large your year-around staff, someone needs to take control of the transition time. We happen to have a director of retreats. She ensures that everyone and everything is ready for her first post-summer camp retreat. If you are a four staff camp and everyone is fully occupied up to their gills, you had better find a very organized volunteer woman to be your transition queen, a.k.a.-T.Q! Her title is important— as queen, she can move and shake people to get things done!

The T.Q. works with the cooks to review the retreat menus. She works with all housekeepers to point out piles of left-over swimsuits and the growing number of cobwebs in the corners of the doorways. She is into the nitty-gritty details that transform summer camps into retreat and conference centers. (This is such an important position I would be advertising the need for this position in newsletters, church visits, and in correspondence sent out to the parents of summer campers!) Trust me... there is a GROUP of ladies out there who thrive on this kind of volunteer activity! Offer her child a free week of camp in exchange for her services. The T.Q. gets the camp ready for adults! This position truly deserves a crown. If done properly, she will have you set up for a great retreat season.

If your retreat business feels stunted, the lack of a proper transition from summer camp to adult guest groups could be the reason. You are trying to handle children and adults with the same systems, the same approach, the same food, the same beds, the same level of cleanliness. It won't work. You will be stuck in stunted position until you change your ways.

I believe most camps over-rate themselves. We all love what we do and we all think we do the best job at what we do. When we hear critics voice concerns we are quick to say, "They don't understand how we do things around a camp." Excuses are made. Blame gets put onto someone else. The guest group comes once, but they won't come again.

T.J. Addington writes in his blog, *Leading from the Sandbox*, "Ministries are not good at evaluation, generally. If in fact, we don't honestly evaluate, it is not really important to us!" Ouch!

I visit many camps. I read many websites. I have heard and read, "We have great, home cooked meals for our retreats." But when I am invited to stay for lunch— after being presented with commercially made corn dogs, sterile looking potato rounds, a container of pre-made apple sauce for a salad, and with a store-bought-hard cookie for dessert- I think to myself, "If this is great homemade cooking, I would hate to taste what an average home cooked meal tastes like!" What I just described could pass for an okay summer camp menu for second graders, but never for a retreat.

Honest assessment: few do it often enough. We are afraid someone might tell us we are not up to grade. Restaurants have them: they are called food critics. When a restaurant is written up in the local newspaper with negative comments, they are smart enough to change or they will eventually go out of business. Let me encourage you to find a "fussy" critic to come to camp and evaluate your food and facilities for a weekend. Give her and her family a free weekend while there are retreats going on in full swing. You might not like what she tells you, but you are going to like her telling you her insights in private, instead of your guest groups telling their world of how they were treated or what they ate or how dirty your buildings were when they arrived at your "conference center!" Unhappy adults become "terrorists" who openly throw opinion bombs out to every listening ear around the water cooler at work or worse yet, on their Facebook postings. They are all aimed back at your camp; the camp who needs repeat business instead of repeater-like complaints.

Listen and respond; let the critic be the impetus for improvement.

## *Points to Ponder*

1. Who can we recruit to be the T.Q.?

2. If I went to another camp, would I like sleeping in this room? What things in our rooms add to our guests' experience while at camp? What things would be considered a hindrance in our rooms?

3. Do we only talk about our great food and facility, or do we worry about every detail and how it will affect our adult retreat groups?

4. Do we use a comment card that gives us immediate feedback from our guests?

5. Where do I find the crown for the T.Q?

*Be ready in season and out of season...*
*2 Timothy 4:2b*

*(My personal exegesis!)*

## CHAPTER 15

# 24/7/365— A Healthy Business Model for Camps

**M**any camps have no imagination. They are creative thinkers when it comes to programs; they just have no imagination on how to generate more revenue. They don't understand the business side of their ministry.

Like it or not, revenue equals momentum: if you have positive revenue you usually have positive momentum. If you're broke, you're broke. Broke is not a fun position to be in. It is no more spiritual to be broke and with no hope than to have a positive cash flow with all the bills paid in full.

## This almost sounds CARNAL!

Many of us want to run the camp in a spiritually purposed way— so we think we can't talk too much about the business side of the camp. I happen to think just the opposite. I want to think so much about the business side of camp that the ministry side has so many more opportunities to be successful. I want the ministry side of camp to flourish.

I want boys and girls to come to know Christ every summer. I want our retreat guests to return home on Sunday renewed in mind and spirit. I want the camp to be sustainable until the Lord comes and takes us home. Therefore, I think about the business side of camp— every day!

How does one build the business side of camp? What does it take to intentionally build the business up to create a level of sustainability? Why would we go to all the work of building or maintaining a camp, if we at the same time don't create systems to allow it to flourish and live on after we are gone or retired?

For me, this is what sorts out the committed worker from the job holders. Job holders are those who like the idea of being in ministry– they like the prestige, the position— but they lack the stick-to-it-tiveness that can actually raise a camp from being the stale, stagnant, stunted camp that merely exists into something great. Their camp is still doing ministry— but there is a lack of passion and drive– they are actually "playing" at doing camp.

Those are harsh words, I know. But sometimes we need to hear it. We need to hear that if we are not putting in 100% of our God-given ability, we shouldn't expect to receive back 100%. Our return can only be as high as our investment of time and energy.

I like to use the term "build" the retreat business. Much of my context is shaped by our particular model at the camp I am currently serving: we have summer camps for kids, and we have a year around retreat ministry serving youth groups, families, and adults. I would make the assumption that most other camps do something very similar— the exception would be the camp that just does a summer camp ministry and locks up the doors before school starts.

For most, summer camp is everything. Much of what we do revolves on getting summer camp right. We know that we have a short window to make a spiritual impact on children under the age of 18. We know that our efforts of putting on summer camp produce much fruit. This is the most exciting part of working at camp– seeing kids come to know Christ.

However, all of us know it takes a huge amount of effort to produce summer camp: countless hours of labor, countless hours of planning, countless hours of promotions and hiring. It takes money to produce a great summer camp. There are a few camps that are able to charge enough to cover all the expenses of summer camp. They have the reputation– a KanaKuk Kamp– so it's easy to put a high price tag on their summer camp experience.

This is not true for most of us. We charge what we think the market will bear. Some camps are charging $150 per week, while others charge $600 per week. There are all ranges of prices in between for a week of summer camp. Each individual camp compares the prices of other camps nearby to determine an average as to what the market will bear: however, this never reflects the actual cost of camp.

In spite of the financial loss, we allow this business decision, knowing that much fruit will be produced during the summer and it is worth it. This is why a great business model needs to be in place. The retreat season should supplement and offset the summer camp expenses. My math still indicates if summer camp expenses exceed summer camp income, one should build up retreat income in order to make up the difference.

For some, their business plan is simple: at the end of the summer they send out a plea looking for more gifts to make up for the shortfall. That is a plan; I just don't like having to rely on it. I like to be a bit more proactive and build the retreat business into something that generates extra dollars, so we can partially underwrite and enhance our summer camp ministry.

Instead of pleading for a donation, we build our calendar.

For the first 18 years we let the guest groups build our calendar for us. We waited until they called us before we filled up the calendar. We let them book four lodges, when in reality they only needed two. We let them decide which weekends they wanted; they built our calendar. It worked. We stayed full— but sometimes we had unused rooms or even unused lodges.

Twelve years ago, we began to change. It was gradual; we began to take more control of the calendar. We had enough history to begin to ask some questions of the guest groups. Christina, our adult ministries director, will suggest, "We see you have booked four lodges the last several year which sleeps 275 people, and you only brought 150 people. How can we help you put your group into three lodges instead of four lodges?" When we did business this way– we freed up a lodge to rent to another group.

Guest groups usually over exaggerate the number of guests they eventually will bring. They are praying and hoping that everyone comes, but when reality sets in, only half of the church will attend their family camp. The camp gets left holding the bag due to unfulfilled expectations of the retreat coordinator. By taking control, we enable two groups to use our facilities instead of just one; we begin to maximize our guest group usage.

The second thing we did was to make sure our larger groups were booked far in advance. Even before they attended this year's retreat, we begin to discuss their needs for next year. We are out in front by building our calendar with groups of 400 first, and then filling the holes with smaller groups. When you don't do this, you eliminate the options of booking a retreat of 300 because you have tied up the buildings with four groups of 20 each. So much of the business is pure math— nothing more, nothing less.

A third way we build our calendar is to wait until four to six months out; then we develop a retreat ourselves to fill any open hole in our calendar. We don't want any open weekends. We have several retreats we are interested in testing out on our constituency. The retreats are theme specific: golf retreat, mother-daughter horse riding retreat, motorcycle ride retreat. These are retreats that we don't know if they will be successful; some are and some aren't.

I made a mistake a few years ago. I wanted to have a father/son big jamboree type of retreat in August. I penciled in the whole camp thinking we were going to attract a huge crowd. By May, we were getting more calls about booking the camp for that weekend I had penciled in for the father/son event. Building by building I released, so that we could book an additional retreat. By late July, I had only one building allocated to this father/son retreat. I never did have the retreat; no interest or bad timing on my part. What I thought was going to be a big hit— ended up being a big flop. Lesson learned: don't overestimate perceived interest when you first start a new retreat.

Little experimental retreats can blossom. Our first sportsmen's retreat had 60 men– today we have 500 men attend— but it was built up over the years by slow and steady growth. Had we not experimented on an open weekend (a hole in the calendar), we would never have stumbled onto the best programmed weekend of the year. We also experienced the opposite: our golf retreat. It was well received the first year– 30 attended. By the third year, it was at 25 attendees- there was no fourth year; we tried, it didn't grow— we eliminated it.

We build our calendar with a 24/7/365 day mindset. There are no days we won't allow a guest group to use us. Period! We book our groups and then we figure out how we will manage it later. We never turn down groups thinking we might be too exhausted or that the flip will be too intense. If we can't physically manage the retreat ourselves, we can bring in extra help.

Why do we push ourselves? Why do we overload our calendar and keep guests on the grounds every day of the year?

The answer is easy: We remember what retreats allows us to do; we remember the faces of children when they announce, "I accepted Christ as my Savior." We remember hearing the late night clang of the bell declaring "a new name has been written in His book of Life."

It is easy to say "yes" when a retreat group wants to book us on Thanksgiving or Christmas day. It is easy when we have guests over Easter- we remember what we are here for. We remember- summer camp.

24/7/365— it is not a job... *it is a way of life.*

## *Points to Ponder*

1. Who controls the calendar in our camp?

2. Do we want to open up the camp to be so busy that everyone is on the run day in and day out?

3. Is part of our stunted position due to our attitude about allowing guest groups to come on the "inconvenient days?"

4. What staff would be needed in order to enlarge our vision for what possibly could be added business, which would supplement our summer ministry?

5. What holes do we allow to remain open in our calendar? What retreats could we create to fill these holes and to create additional revenue?


*As long as it is day, we must do the work of him who sent me.*
*Night is coming, when no one can work.*

*John 9:4*

## CHAPTER 16
# Everybody Knows Something About Everything

I never like to be caught shorthanded. Staff gets sick. Staff goes on vacation. Staff is caught up on finishing a building before it snows. Sometimes, staff quit their jobs.

I solved that problem: everybody knows something about everything. It is a simple concept. Whatever your job description states you will do— we add more to it; not permanently, but just like the temp a business would hire for a day. We allow our staff to help out for an hour, for a day, for a week until the job is finished or an absent staff member returns to work. Some love the variety— there is resistance from others.

We allow office people to mow if their work is caught up. We allow kitchen staff to help us install a tongue and groove wood ceiling during their slow month of December; we know they want hours prior to Christmas. We allow house-keepers to paint when their rooms are all clean and there are days still left in the week. We allow maintenance staff to come to the office and help stuff envelopes when a major bulk mailing must be in the mail yesterday.

Did you hear the word? *We allow!*

Why would we do this? We insist that everyone works with efficiency and focus; it is part of our culture to stay busy. We are paying a staff person to put in a full week; why not allow them each to work efficiently the entire week? We already know our current staff. It is much easier to give our staff directions rather than train an outside person. An outsider would not know where the maintenance shed or a particular building is located. Our staff can do it faster, with more care, and have a sense of ownership by the completion of their temp job.

Not only is it efficient, it is actually a team building activity that produces tangible results. I am not against trust falls and rope course activity. I just find nothing tangible gets accomplished there. Everybody gets a little warm fuzzy out of the activity; I have seen very few lasting results for our efforts on the challenge courses. When an office girl, a kitchen girl, a maintenance boy, and the construction director installs 2500 square feet of tongue and groove finished pine boards onto a new ceiling– there is actual bonding and teamwork going on. The maintenance staff gets to know the kitchen staff. The office girl gets to know the construction crew. Bethany learns to trust Joylyn as she holds the ladder in place. Do you see the picture? This is real TEAM WORK! Emphasis on WORK!

An additional benefit of everyone doing everything: we get a lot done— fast! We build a new building every year; it is our goal to have it fully enclosed before the first snow.

Sometimes we are early. Often times the wind is strong and cold as we put on the last piece of siding. When there is pressure to accomplish something, everybody who can drops what they are doing and helps out another department. The same is true when the housekeepers have a three hour window to flip one of our buildings between back-to-back retreats– everyone jumps in and helps. Many hands make light work. When the kitchen is serving a 1000 plate company picnic supper– everyone becomes proficient at something in the kitchen– yep, even the maintenance boys.

We want every staff member to take ownership in their jobs. We don't want them to engage in an entrenchment mentality. We don't let them use first person words such as: I, me, or my; it is always we or us. We don't allow an attitude that tells everyone else, "I shall not be moved. I am too important, too fragile, too smart, too dumb, too fat, too skinny to do anything more than what I am currently doing right now." My answer always will be, "Yes You Can!"

I love it when Paige comes into the office, and with a smile on her face says, "I showed my husband how to sheet rock our kitchen last night." She knows we have taught her a life-skill that will be of value for every house she ever owns; her husband is not so wild about it though. We just created a little firecracker and he now has to keep up with her!

I treat everyone equally. I have the same expectation for each staff; we all pitch in until the job is done– done well indeed!

## *Points to Ponder*

1. What jobs are there at camp that everyone should be allowed to work?

2. What dynamics would change in staff relationships if everyone was encouraged to help other departments when in need?

3. What are the drawbacks of staff being multi-functional?

4. Will this work with a staff of two or three? Why or why not?

5. How do we decide who gets to leave the office to mow on the first day of spring?

*And though a man might prevail against one who is alone, two will withstand him—*
*a threefold cord is not quickly broken.*

*Ecclesiastes 4:12*

## CHAPTER 17

# Praying on the Run

At times, I have been accused of acting unspiritual. New staff will accuse me of not having enough organized prayer times together during our busy summer months.

Here is my answer: "Put your tennis shoes on sister, we are going to pray on the run."

We are going to pray on the run as we jump on the backhoe and head to the leaking hydrant, "Help me Lord I don't know what I'm doing." We are going to pray on the run when we are driving to town because the bread truck doesn't show with buns for lunch, "Help me Lord, I hope someone has 300 hot dog buns." We are going to pray on the run as we drive the van loaded down with Jr. High boys to the river with a rack full of canoes, "Help them Lord, for they know not what they are doing." We are going to pray on the run to the 7 a.m. summer staff meeting, weary and unprepared, "Lord help me for I know not what to say."

The new staff member gets the picture after a while and returns to her desk— and she begins to pray, "Help him Lord, because he REALLY is in over his head."

And HE does!

## Points to Ponder

1. When am I praying?

2. In what things have I seen the Lord answer my prayers miraculously this past year?

3. When will I ever get to have a real prayer meeting with staff?

4. How can we instill the "praying on the run" principle in all the staff during the busy summer months?

5. Can we set up a praying system on our smart phones so all can be notified when there is a need for concentrated prayer by all staff?

*Pray without ceasing.*
*I Thessalonians 5:7*

# CHAPTER 18
# Managing Without Understanding

Many directors are placed in positions of over-seeing many different functions and disciplines of the camp. This is usually the case unless you are working for an extremely large camp with layers and layers of supervisors overseeing the different departments. In camps with under 10 full time staff, the director is forced to be the one that every department head reports to: there is no middle-line supervisor who shields a director from day to day operations.

I thrive on this type of system! If I had been stuck in the office for eight hours a day— pushing paper from one side of the desk to the other, staring blankly into the computer screen, or being forced to attend or lead countless "meetings," I would have not survived the 35 years I have been in camping. I love to walk around.

In the 80's there was a buzz methodology of "managing by walking around," promoted by Tom Peters and Robert Waterman in their book, *In Search of Excellence.* 30 years later, I am still walking around. It appears to be the way

I operate camp the best. I want to keep my hand on the pulse of all workers; I want to see that they are working in their "sweet spot." I want to see that they are moving ahead on a project. I want to give them a vision of what the next project could look like. I like to be with staff and know how their job functions.

When I walk around I see that the housekeepers need a new laundry cart on wheels to put dirty towels in. I see that the shop foreman needs a new vice. I see the kitchen struggling to function without enough convection ovens. I see too long of lines on the carpet ball tables. When I return to the office, I can make an educated decision to purchase a cart, a vice, an oven, and to build three more carpet ball tables. I am not relying on middle management people to relay to me the needs of the staff. I see; then I order!

This system also eliminates unnecessary purchases. I have seen store rooms of items not in use today that were bought because someone squeaked the loudest by saying "we need this item!" Walking around helps a camp director make better decisions about what is really a "need" and which ones are "want" items.

You need to know for a reason: it is because YOU NEED TO KNOW! AND YOU NEED TO KNOW IT SOONER THAN LATER! This is probably going to be more of a need for the newbie director: the rookie, the beginner; the one who is in charge, but has no idea what he is doing. Pay attention! A little understanding about a lot of things will serve you well for years to come.

## *Points to Ponder*

1. As a newbie director, in which area am I weak in understanding?

2. Do I really need to know what goes on in the kitchen or maintenance shed?

3. I went to school and studied finance or management— what does knowing how an oven works matter to me?

4. How do I walk around without meddling in the business of other staff?

5. Will the cook give me a fresh baked cookie if I walk through the kitchen at 11 a.m.?

*Blessed is the man who WALKS in the ways*
*of the righteous;*
*whatever he does will prosper*

*Psalms 1:1*

## CHAPTER 19
# Know the Kitchen

A round 15% of your operating budget is getting eaten up in the dining room; you need to know your kitchen. What do I mean "know" the kitchen? I mean KNOW the kitchen- intimately. This is the one place that large amounts of money can be wasted foolishly and you, the director, are clueless. This is the one spot in the budget you can shave 2% off and reap a sizable reward.

- Know how many staff are actually needed to produce a meal for 50, or 75, or 250. Create a formula that lets the lead cook know she can have two helpers and a dishwasher when she is cooking for 150 guests. Know when one helper is enough. Know when the cook can do it all.

- Know what is in season and why apples need to be served in the fall, oranges around Christmas, grapes in February and strawberries in May and June. Know what it costs per serving.

- Know what each plate costs you to produce. Know that you can buy a store bought hamburger bun for 22 cents or buy a frozen whole wheat bun that bakes up fresh-like, for 23 cents.

- Know that the government reimburses you for the milk served to children.

- Know how the automatic dish washer operates and occasionally jump in and help the 15-year-old who is overwhelmed by the huge pile of pots and pans.

- Know the tilting skillet, know the convection oven, and know the 30 quart mixer. Know how to operate them. Know where the switches, the off button, the temperature regulators are located. Be able to lend a hand with skill when the cook falls behind.

- Know how to serve up desserts and dish ice cream out on the line.

- Know how to use the gas grill for burger, hot dogs, steaks, and chicken.

- Know where the cereal is located, the bowls and cups, the plastic spoons, and sugar packets. Make yourself useful over the breakfast hour.

- Know how to make coffee, reload the juice machine, and refill the pop dispensing machine when the boxes of syrup run dry.

- Know the difference in cuts of meats: what an inside round looks like, what center cut pork chops cost, and that chicken breasts can be purchased as 5 oz or

6 oz or 8 oz servings, adjusting accordingly, depending on the size of your guests' girth and appetite.

- Know what food is being thrown away by guests; work the dish return line and watch what comes back from the table on plates. See that the cooks adjust the menu accordingly.

- Know how much food is wasted by cooking excessively and not according to a formula that calculates quantity of food that is needed for the actual number of guests.

- Know how to cook breakfast when the cook is sick or oversleeps.

- Know how to make popcorn the old-fashion way— on top of the stove.

I want to know all that because I sign the check to Sysco and Martin Brothers. **I need to know!** And so do you!

## *Points to Ponder*

1. Knowing that food is the backbone of the camp, why don't more of our staff members understand how the kitchen works and where equipment is located?

2. How many is too many people to have in the loop of the kitchen operation?

3. How do our kitchen staff and bookkeeper work hand in hand in communicating expenditures and invoices? Who monitors the kitchen's spending habits?

4. Does the director really need to know how to cook breakfast for 40?

5. Where are the plastic spoons located?

*But he said to them,*
*"You give them something to eat."*
*They said, "We have no more than*
*five loaves and two fish—*
*unless we are to go and buy food*
*for all these people."*

*Luke 9:13*

# CHAPTER 20
# Know the Maintenance Shop

I am a former grounds keeper/maintenance man, so this comes easy for me. I know where things are and I usually know how to fix it. However, if you are more comfortable in the office than on a tractor, you still need to know most of the following list:

- You need to know the difference in function between a 12" Miter saw and an 8" saw.

- You need to know why the camp buys 18 volt Dewalt cordless drills and not 14 volt.

- You need to know how to turn on the gas barrels.

- You need to know where the keys are to all tractors.

- You need to know how to set up a table saw.

- You need to know the difference between #2 grade lumber and #3 grade lumber.

- You need to know when to use OSB, construction grade plywood, or marine grade plywood.

- You need to know the difference between .40 and .60 treated lumber and when and where to use each.

- You need to know when to use stainless steel, galvanized or common nails.

- You need to know how to check the oil in all the mowers.

- You need to know how to mix the 2 cycle oil with gas at the right mixture rate.

- You need to know how to restring a weed whip.

- You need to know how to grade a road, plow snow, and dig a ditch.

- You need to know what size culverts go in particular drainage areas.

- You need to know what tree will grow in wet areas or what will grow in a dry area.

- You need to know the difference of function between a 16" chain saw and a 24" chain saw.

- You need to know where the extra light bulbs are located.

- You need to know how to jump a car with a dead battery.

- You need to know how to hook up a battery charger and how many amps to use for a slow or fast charge.

- You need to know how to plug a leaky tire, where the supplies are kept, and know how to turn on the air compressor.

- You need to know where the paint, brushes, sand paper and rollers are stored.

Why do I need to know all this? I might be the only one around on a Saturday night at 10:30 when a guest's car won't start. I need to know this when a light is out on a pathway. I need to know when the front door on the lodge is broken while a group is in camp— and the maintenance man is out of camp. I want to know so I can solve the problems: FIX IT NOW and not later. The guests will be gone later!

## *Points to Ponder*

1. How do I turn on the air compressor?

2. Do our guests feel cared for by our staff when problems arise with their vehicles?

3. Can we have a training hour at the maintenance shed for all staff and serve our lunch there too?

4. Why does it matter if we fix burned out light bulbs when a guest group is on the grounds?

*I must work the works of him that sent me,*
*while it is day: the night cometh,*
*when no man can work.*

*John 9:4*

# CHAPTER 21
## Know the Program Areas

I am not a program type of guy; some would consider me a bit too serious to be too much fun at playing games and doing activities. However, my intenseness about my work does not keep me from wanting to know how the program areas work. I want to know if they are safe. I want to see if there are inefficient systems in their operation. I want to know that the staff is handling the guests with the right attitude. I intentionally get out of the office and go and watch our guests do activities. Here is a list of things that directors need to know:

- Know the rules for carpet ball, gaga pit, and 9-square— and all the variations of the rules!

- Know how much the blob costs to have refurbished and how often it gets refurbished.

- Know how to repair a paddle boat and what parts should be on hand to make the repairs.

- Know how an air-soft gun works.

- Know what craft projects are being made and the expense and the profit of each project!

- Know how to put on a climbing harness.

- Know how to string up a bow and load up a bb gun.

- Know how to start a fire, cook a meal with a Dutch oven and how to store the Dutch oven when you are finished using it.

- Know where drop off and pick up points are for the canoes on the river.

- Know how to string up a fishing pole, bait a hook, and how to clean a fish.

- Know how to saddle a horse, feed a horse, and know where the trails are that horses and riders travel upon.

- Know how to set up a tent.

- Know how to fix a swing, a slide, or a glider.

- Know where extra horse shoes are located.

- Know where the new ping pong paddles are located, where extra pool balls can be found, and where extra foosballs are hidden.

- Know how to lower the baskets in the gym, set up the volleyball nets, and where the dodge balls are located.

- Know where the toboggans are stored, and how to run the toboggan run.

The list goes on and on. Just prepare yourself to know how all things work. You are able to plan and adjust quicker when someone is gone, and you happen to be the last person in camp.

## *Points to Ponder*

1. Where are the extra carpet balls, horseshoes, and ping pong balls kept?

2. Who is responsible to make sure all program areas are ready for our retreat groups?

3. Is there a system in place to ensure that staff regularly does maintenance on the fun areas of camp?

4. Is there a central depot for all program equipment, or is it strung all over camp in closets and out buildings?

5. What will it take to get our program equipment organized and in one place?

*Now may the God who gives perseverance*
*and encouragement*
*grant you to be of the same mind with one another*
*according to Christ Jesus.*

*Romans 15:5*

## Chapter 22

# Deliver the Goods

ewarding staff can be tricky. There are staff members who constantly amaze you with their performance and there are others whom you are constantly redirecting– with a cattle prod. The two staff members appear to be from completely different worlds.

I treat everyone differently. Some will say, "That isn't fair!" I say, "It isn't my job to be **fair**: it is my job to *get it right!*"

Glenn Brooke from *Leadership Craft* writes this: "What matters is what gets delivered, shipped, and produced. Some people need neat and organized to get stuff accomplished, and others don't. There are professional contexts for workplaces where your preferences don't weigh much (e.g., no clutter or tripping hazards in a factory, every tool is carefully cleaned and in its place in the auto repair shop, or your company has a clean desk policy to limit the loss of intellectual property). What counts is the output. We should get paid for what we produce."

Brooke continues, "Some of us work in organizations where far too many rewards and promotions go to individuals who didn't produce anything useful, but they followed all the rules and filled out all the forms on time and didn't offend anyone. They didn't advance the business in any positive sense, but also didn't show up on any critic's radar, so hey, 3% raise and yeah, they're in line for a promotion because it's been three years since their last one. Don't be that person. As a leader, don't create a culture that supports those people."

And I don't!

Occasionally during staff meetings someone will voice a complaint: they think the flower bed looks terrible, or that the inside of the work trucks should be kept cleaner. I always ask, "Is that a burden? Let me assign you to that task!" Talk is cheap, but it is those who deliver the goods who will get the reward.

There are many things that I look for in a young employee. The character trait that rises to the top is initiative: initiative is responding to a need before a guest even knows she needs help; initiative is anticipating the need of a ladder before one is needed; initiative is the drive to start up a project or a program that will enhance the ministry, all the while knowing it will cause the employee more work. I reward initiative. I promote initiative. I fire lazy.

I pay employees a salary for their value; not for the position. I don't pay a higher salary because they have nine kids and a big mortgage. Each person gets paid according to their output. Some want to be rewarded on a seniority basis; I will promote a rookie over a lazy, unimaginative long-term staff member. I believe I need to pay for back and intellectual power; both are necessary– some staff lack one or both.

Camps can be one of the more guilty parties in hiring: we hire those "who need a job" or the ones for whom "it will be good to be around other Christians." And on the other side of the spectrum, camps can be slow to let go of staff who are not "delivering the goods." Directors think that staff members are family, and you don't fire family. One of the reasons camps become stunted is they are not firing quickly enough.

I have seen this in my camp. I have made some bad hires of people who were in need of a job. I paid for it after six months. There was a REAL reason why they were without a job. They either had skill set issues, or they had no relational skills; they are unable to get along with the other staff or carry their own water.

Our younger staff often complains about not being moved up fast enough, especially when they see a peer getting moved up through the system with more pay and more responsibilities. When I discover their concerns, I always approach them with this question, "What have you done in the last 90 days to enhance yourself– to add value to yourself– so that you have become so valuable to our organization that we can't live without you?"

Just showing up and punching in is not enough.

Flexibility, availability, manageability equals great attitude... 75% of what a person does is perceived by their attitude.

I purposely give random raises to deserving staff. I don't wait until the end-of-the-year. When a staff is knocking it out of the ball park every week with extra initiatives— I want to reward him. When a staff is thinking and working at building the business— I want to reward her. Rewarded achievement multiplies itself over and over again. The camp is always rewarded with a more energized staff person, who wants to continue to grow and blossom into a better staff person, when they are fairly rewarded.

Who is delivering the goods? Who are all talk and no show? Who needs released today so that they can go work elsewhere?

## *Points to Ponder*

1. Are there staff members on our team that are not pulling their weight?

2. In what areas are we having to "carry other people's water" for them in order for them to keep their job?

3. What are the clear standards of performance that must be accomplished by each staff member?

4. Do we have a system in place that allows instant rewards instead of year-end rewards?

5. How do we bring the young staff along into being productive members of our camping team?

*And let us not lose heart in doing good,*
*for in due time we shall reap*
*if we do not grow weary.*

*Galatians 6:9*

## CHAPTER 23
# The Surprise: The Gary Factor

**W**e all have felt it! You know; the surprise of someone thinking so much about you and for you that they bring you something un-expected– a gift, a pie, a plate of their last night's supper for you to enjoy for lunch: acts of kindness, randomly given to you, that nearly bring you to tears.

We attended a CCCA sectional conference a few years ago at Lake Geneva Camps and Conferences in Wisconsin. Our staff was all excited about going to a nice camp in a nice location. I stayed behind in order to perform the funeral for a friend's wife. When they returned, they didn't talk about the speaker, or the beds, or the seminars. They talk-ed about Gary.

Gary was the cook. Gary cooked a good meal for the staff and they were served well. The staff was content- their ex-pectation level was met. But what Gary did beyond just cooking and serving was what impacted our staff. Gary walked through the dining room greeting guests, interact-ing with eye contact and touch. Our staff loved that kind of attention and rose to the occasion by creating a spirited dialog with Gary. One young staff member commented jokingly, "I wish I could have had some ice cream." The dialog ended, the staff returned to their normal conversation around the table, and Gary returned to his kitchen.

But here is where the memorable gift developed that Gary gave to our staff. He returned to our staff's table with a simple bowl of ice cream, hand dipped and loaded with toppings, by Gary himself, and presented it to Ryan with a smile and a touch to the shoulder! WOW! We no longer talk about extra care by mentioning it randomly; we now call it the **Gary Factor!**

You want to build your retreat business? You want momentum? Enact the Gary factor principle.... Random acts of kindness given with a smile and a personal touch create legends. Just ask our staff!

## *Points to Ponder*

1. Does our staff have the "Gary" factor?

2. How do we give our staff permission to implement the "Gary" factor?

3. How can our staff learn this attitude?

4. Do our guests receive enough "random acts of kindness?"

5. How can we hire Gary for our camp?

*Be kind to one another...*
*Ephesians 4:32a*

## CHAPTER 24

# When You're Here, You're Family— Keep Your Rules Simple

**W**e have two rules we regularly enforce: keep your pets out of our buildings and leave your booze and other addictive material at home. If you are not violating someone else's space or putting yourself in danger, we don't say much; we leave our guests alone.

I like to operate from the position of, "YES you CAN", rather from the position of "NO you CAN'T." Guests feel that freedom; they feel at home! Staff are empowered to "let" guests feel at home— the feeling of being able to put your feet up on the coffee table without fear of a reprimand; the feeling of being able to raid the refrigerator when the munchies attack; the feeling of knowing it is okay to track in mud and make messes. *"Relax... when you are here with us... you're family!"*

Never do we refer to a manual when asked by a guest group if they can do something. We know in our hearts, the answer will be yes! When we are asked, "Can we move the 400 chairs out of the chapel so we can have an event?" "Yes!" "Can we bring a tent and set it up on the grassy area to hold a chapel for 700?" "Yes... and you can use our bobcat to help pound in the stakes."— "Can we have 40 picnic tables set up near the climbing wall and big swing for an afternoon picnic?"— "Yes, and we will make you 20 dozen chocolate chip cookies also to go with your sack lunch at no charge!"

We have all flown from major airports. Before we finally get settled into our seats we feel infringed upon. We have been prodded, poked, and photographed; they have their rules and they enforce them. We don't feel the love. We don't feel like family to the TSA... we feel like the enemy.

Camps with excessive regulations and rigid procedures give their guests the same feeling: the TSA treatment! And you are wondering why you are stunted? Is it any wonder you are not first choice when a group coordinator begins the retreat planning process back at the local church? We prefer to be the grandma instead of the gatekeeper. We prefer to be the enabler rather than the watchman. We prefer to be generous rather than being stingy and miserly. We want to be the guests' agent instead of being their roadblock.

I recently visited with Tim, a youth pastor who told me of his experience when utilizing another camp: "We couldn't do anything without asking permission. We couldn't set up the stage the way we wanted- they didn't want to move their piano. We wanted lunch at 11:30- they told us it had to be at noon. We wanted to play dodge ball at midnight- they told us the gym was closed and locked at 11 p.m. I am glad we could come back home to your camp." And they never have left!

Rules are necessary: Don't jump off the tower or zip line without a harness! Don't ride backwards on your horse! Don't be blobbing without a life jacket! Don't play paintball without a mask! Those are safety issues: they must be enforced with an iron fist- there is no compromise.

When I was a child, I had two aunts whom we visited often; one I loved and one— I only went because I was forced to go. One opened up her home and let us run, let us eat, let us play without a lot of fussing— we felt perfectly at home there. The other, her furniture was covered with the clear plastic, there were rooms in the house we were not even allowed to walk into, and her meal time rations were meager at best! Which auntie do I love to talk about, tell my friends about? The one who made me feel at home.

Your guests will feel the same way.

It starts at the first point of contact with the office staff who takes the reservation or who processes the registrations as they arrive in the mail. We have trained Michelle intentionally to answer, "Yes, we can do that. Yep, that is easy to do! Not a problem, we will handle that for you. Sure, midnight is not too late to have s'mores ready for you." I have told the staff the only time I want to hear the words NO, is when a youth pastor asks, "Can our youth group of 30 sleep overnight on top of the climbing tower?" And even then I would want them to say, "No, but you can sleep at the base of the tower!"

This same mentality must pervade all departments. The kitchen has to be ready with alternatives and be willing to offer them. I love it when I hear Kristen, our food service director, respond to a request from a gluten-free guest,

"Sure, we can cook you a chicken breast; is there anything else that we can get you?" Or when a guest forgets to bring sleeping bags, pillows or tooth paste, and Paige from guest services replies, "Will two pillows be enough? Here is an extra blanket in case you get cold— and here are extra towels... and no charge ma'am, glad to help!" Or when Rachelle, the food service coordinator, sets out styrofoam leftover containers next to the extra cookies or cinnamon rolls with a note, "Please take some home for your family— you enjoyed them— so will they!" It comes easy, it comes natural, it is ingrained into their DNA— respond with love, care, and become generous; your guests will feel it and will love you back.

Do we do this in all departments? All departments! Even the maintenance department has to have the generous spirit about them. When there is a flat tire, Dale will fix it if he can. If a battery is dead, Brett will charge it. If a car is locked with the keys in the ignition; Matt will break in. And... no charge ma'am!

Why do we do this? Why do we give away the farm, if needed, in order to accommodate our guest groups? It is a Biblical principle, but it is also a simple business decision: we want our guests to feel so good about their time with us that they want to keep coming back for more.

We want repeat customers. We want repeat customers who bring their friends and family back the next time they come. We want families to grow to love us so much they want to bring their entire extended family reunion to camp. It is a ripple effect that is started when a staff person offers random, generous acts of kindness to a guest who is in need of a towel, a piece of gluten-free chicken, or air in their tires.

You can call it love or care or hospitality. Call it what you want: Just Do It!

## *Points to Ponder*

1. Does each staff member know they have the ability to meet the immediate needs of any guests regardless of the price? Is there a limit?

2. Does the office staff know how to say yes?

3. What are the times when someone can say NO to a guest?

4. How do we convince even the stingiest to be generous with their goods, their service and their talents?

5. What will it take to turn our camp into "home?"

<br>

*One gives freely, yet grows all the richer;*
*another withholds what he should give,*
*and only suffers want.*

*Proverbs 11:24*

## Chapter 25
# Don't Take Yourself Too Seriously

*Laugh at yourself— laugh with others.*
*Where there is no laughter— there is no fun.*
*Where there is no fun— everything becomes work.*
*When it is all work— you sweat.*
*When you sweat— you grow weary.*
*When you grow weary— you quit.*

Lighten up, friend. Don't take yourself so seriously. According to Greek mythology, Atlas grew weary of holding the skies on his shoulders: what makes you think you can carry the entire load yourself— all the time?

I have done many things over the years to lighten my load— I too have grown weary of holding up the operation of the camp. I too wanted to remove the burden from my back. I too have ended the summer fatigued beyond recognition.

Here are a few ways to keep laughing instead of growing weary:

- Take a vacation; take as many vacations as you can. When our children were small, and we were poor, we loaded up the tent and just left camp. It didn't matter where we went, as long as there was distance between us and the day-to-day operation. I used to tell the staff, "Don't call me unless a building burns down." Luckily, I received no calls.

- Don't act too smart! I mean it! Don't act like you know it all about everything at camp! Here is why: when you act cocky and sure of yourself, you set yourself up to get your knees knocked out from beneath you. However, when you look and act just a bit "stupid," everything you do is a pleasant surprise to those you serve! By not acting or dressing like the "brightest" bulb, people are shocked when you actually hit the switch and POW! You blow their socks off! I like to dress like the garbage man and act like the CEO!

- Get a hobby! A serious hobby that you are nearly addicted to. I chose hunting and fishing. There are two months a year that I bow hunt– serious bow hunting– like– every-day-bow-hunting. I hunt until I am successful. Some years my season is shorter than others. Does my work suffer during my preoccupation with shooting Bambi's father? It probably does to a certain extent! Here is what it does for me: I am able to have time to think, to plan in my head, to ponder the ministry of camp, to step back and get perspective. I forget today's operation. I give myself time to anticipate the future. I can't get think-time while worrying about food preparations, or worrying about having the lawn mowed, or thinking about if the horses are saddled. A director who does not remove himself from a camp environment will burn out! How have I lasted for 35 years? I have survived by having a life outside of camp.

- Somehow, connect with a church. I remember the years when I needed to be at every retreat, every day, making sure all systems were running smoothly. For those with smaller staffs, it never changes; you are still needed every weekend. But without a church family– you're toast. When there are no moorings in your life that you can hold on to when times get rough and weary– that is when you need your church family. That is when you need a friendly non-camp-person's ear.

- Let your kids work right alongside you. I feel sorry for those who work for camps that won't let family members work together on staff. I understand why boards create this policy; I just find it shortsighted. Families that work alongside each other grow together– instead of apart. Children who are given responsibilities at camp grow up to be outstanding full-time staff members. Moms and Dads trying to run a weekend retreat can receive much joy as they watch their children perform dish washing and learn to serve the guests.

Just as you build your retreat calendar, build your personal calendar. Schedule yourself for vacations, schedule yourself for hobbies; schedule yourself to spend time with your wife and children in such a way that when the kids are gone from the house, you will have no regrets about the amount of time your spent building the ministry.

Fresh, clear-minded staff members remain at camp for longer durations. Longer duration of staff adds continuity to programs and development. Continuity of systems creates momentum and drives the camp into a vibrant ministry that develops into a sustainable movement.

So lighten up... laugh every day!

## *Points to Ponder*

1. How "stupid" do I act?

2. What is the persona that I demonstrate?

3. Am I out of balance when it comes to work and play?

4. Will my children speak highly of their time as "camp kids" or will they only remember the amount of time I was absent taking care of guest needs?

5. What is Carnival Cruise Line's phone number?

*A joyful heart is good medicine,*
*but a crushed spirit dries up the bones.*

*Proverbs 17:22*

CHAPTER **26**

# It's Just Plain Hard Work—
# Preserving the Family

I was born to work. My mother was a worker. My grandfather was a worker. I get extreme satisfaction from finishing a job. I am a driver. I constantly remind those I work with to work with efficiency, with diligence, with purpose, and figure on getting little praise as you are sweating and enduring long days, full weekends, and working most holidays. Welcome to camp, I tell new staff; you just signed up for a job where you're on call, on time, and stay late.

Some fall right in step— they thrive on the activity and the pace. Others don't settle in as well— as a matter of fact, they fight it. It is hard for a new staff member who is new to the camp setting, to readjust his thinking regarding his weekends. His former friends are going to football games on Saturday— he is back at the camp running the tower or finishing up lunch. Her friends are all active in their church, while she is serving a mid-morning Sunday brunch for 200.

If you function best with a job description that is accurate, you might not get along too well in a camp— especially in a small camp. The smaller the camp the more your job description can be boiled down to one word: EVERYTHING— and then some. Rigid, single-minded people should not apply— you will only be frustrated. A.D.D. type of minds works best: focus here for 10 minutes— then to be pulled away on something else that takes a higher priority. There are seldom two days that look alike; there are seldom two hours that look alike. The name of the game is flexibility and adaptability.

Christian camping is one of the easiest doors to enter into full-time ministry; more laymen with specific skills are able to be utilized at a camp than at our local churches. It is better to come in with many disciplines, rather than one specific trade. It comes back to "the more you know", the more valuable you can be to the camp.

Finding the right blend of skills and personalities is difficult: some people are more interested in the ministry side of camp— they love people. While others love to be hidden away constructing a building; they will work with volunteers, but it is not their comfort zone.

Those who prefer to be with people, but have to stay in the shop— are frustrated. Those who want to stay in the shop, but are drug out to help at a program area feel awkward. Getting someone who can slip in and out of different roles is difficult.

What two great character qualities should a director look for when hiring an additional staff member? I would think flexibility is high on the list; being a self-started is another.

I like hiring people with push and drive as well. I would prefer a new staff person who has these basic character traits, rather than a particular skill set. I hire for attitude and train for skills. Morose, self-centered people can suck the life out of the rest of the camp staff. Team players will always work best— lone wolves end up being a constant irritation and a nemesis to others. If a camp staff does not gel well together, a director has additional issues he will have to sort out.

I love being with our staff during the week or on a weekend, but I don't want to socialize with JUST camp people. I want to be comfortable talking about other things than just about camp activity. I don't want to have to rehash the last week and I usually don't want to discuss the work load that is ahead of me.

When I am with non-camp friends I want to talk about everything BUT camp. If I tell a new staff anything at the beginning, I always tell them, "Have a life outside of camp. Develop friends. Somehow get involved in some kind of ministry in the local church or even the local soup line. Create a network of NON camp people. You will survive longer if you do."

Isolation can wear on families involved in camp ministry. Though surrounded by large groups of people, there is still the need for wives to connect on a person-to-person level. During a weekend, there usually is not the time to sit and visit very long or very deep with guests— it is "hellos and quick goodbyes— how you doing?" that make up most of our conversations with guests.

Men who talk their wives into moving to the country in order that they can work at a camp have to be aware they are creating a hole in their family's lives. Men need to make special compensations to allow the family to connect outside the context of camp. "If mama ain't happy– ain't nobody happy," can be the camp family motto!

There is no one way to accomplish the mission of protecting the family. Many families are blown away by the amount of work that is thrust on them when they arrive at camp. Some cannot comprehend why there are so many interruptions to their routine. We grew our family from zero to four while at camp– and they all graduated from high school and left home while at camp– they never knew anything different. Their routine was to have no routine at all. They knew weekends were to be spent working at camp; summers were extra fun because the camp filled up with counselors and other staff; and that there were 660 acres of land to play and run on the rest of the year.

We home schooled our children for their entire schooling years; let me rephrase that– we "tried" to home school our kids. It was a perfect blend of work and school– with an emphasis on the work. Emerson is a teacher, Evie is a caterer, Emily is a missionary in France, and Elly is a very versatile camp worker. They turned out to be adults that love the Lord, are capable in many areas of service, and have much flexibility. They became hard workers.

It is hard work. The hours are long. It is living a lifestyle that is completely different from the rest of your world; but it is also very rewarding if the family can stay balanced throughout their time serving the ministry of the camp.

It is truly a husband and wife team— families that have a mate that is not engaged in the camp life fizzle sooner than later— they simply don't last. For me personally, not only did my wife, DeDe, jump into the ministry and help wherever needed, so did my children. My children were washing camp dishes when they needed a milk crate to stand on to operate the dishwasher. They needed extra weight put on the mower seat to keep it running. They needed a step stool to put a saddle on one of the horses. There were no self-esteem issues in my family— everyone had work to do and they were all needed to keep the ministry going.

Living on the grounds can be a blessing and a curse. Our family loved it; we wanted to be right in the middle of all the action— 24/7. The camp house allowed us to slip in and out of work without ever getting into a car or feel like we were leaving for work— it was natural. We loved that our children could ride their bikes out to a work site to check on dad— or more importantly, could bring dad cold drinks and sandwiches! We loved knowing the kids could walk down to breakfast at the camp dining hall when both of us were working the early morning shift.

But we did set some particular barriers to keep camp from encroaching onto our family: our home was not a flop house for summer staff needing a couch and an air conditioner. Our house was not a buffet line for weekend staff.

Our house and yard were basically off limits to summer staff. Why you ask? I wanted to protect my family time and more importantly not infringe on my wife to clean up and cook for extras— she was not their mother. Parents have to guard the door whenever summer arrives; the open door policy should just be the office door, and not the living room door.

Special attention needs to be paid to the "camp brat" syndrome. Nobody likes the mouthy little guy under our feet or interrupting a counselor with his cabin of boys. Camp staff cannot let their kids run wild. My wife, DeDe, used to tell the counselors during staff training week: "Don't let my kids get in your way— send them home with a kick in the pants if they interfere!" When a kid starts using phrases like, "My dad runs (or owns) this place," you know he has become a "camp brat." We constantly told our children, "We are here to serve... now do likewise and stay out of people's way!"

If you are just getting started in your camping career and your family is young, you are blessed: you are blessed with the opportunity to work alongside your family— guiding and teaching them to serve and to look out for the interests and needs of other people. You are blessed that your children will know and understand what their parents actually do to make a living. You are blessed to build work skills and attitudes into your sons and daughters. You will be blessed to watch your children grow up with wonderful "camp friends" who return every year to reconnect back into your children's lives. You can be blessed that your entire family is engaged in a life-changing ministry.

If you have raised your family at camp— you know what I mean. You understand the wonderful joy of passing the baton on to your children with work opportunities. I watched at Camp Peniel near Marble Falls, Texas, as the retired director, Don Barber, gave me the history of the camp, and proudly pointed to his son, who is now working full-time as the boy's ministry director. Those are priceless rewards for faithful service. All the hard work, the late hours, the interruptions of family life come to a climax once you reach a certain age and you look back at the years and years of service. You will know it is worth it when you see your grandson ride his bike through camp– just as your son did 30 years before.

My advice: work hard; engage all of your family members in the ministry; establish friends away from camp; and stick around long enough that your grandchildren will be blessed by your efforts.

## *Points to Ponder*

1. Am I looking at my time at camp as a career jumping point or as a life time commitment? How long have I committed myself to serving at this camp?

2. How am I protecting my family from some of the craziness of camp life?

3. Does my family feel a part of the ministry? Or do they feel like camp is getting all of me and they are getting the leftovers?

4. Do I have any friends who are not camp people? Why not? Name five non-camp friends.

5. When was the last time my family had a weekend alone without any summer staff sleeping on my couch?

*Greet my dear friend Persis,*
*another woman,*
*who has worked very hard in the Lord.*

*Romans 16:12*

# CHAPTER 27
## ... Good Job!

For the younger director, who works all alone, on the prairie... you are missing the accolades of home and school... there are no "Good Jobs!" You are on your own. You're lonely, and all you do is work. You have pulled your wife out to this rural setting and all you see is peeling paint and dust balls; *"seldom is heard an encouraging word... as the deer and the antelope play"*... you know the tune.

I speak the words "Good Job" very sparingly. I have grown older listening to parents, "good job" their kids right into laziness and the entitlement mentality. I like to say, "Your salad was wonderful and tasty," or, "the dining room is so clean." Praise for doing something good is great. Praise for just being... adds no value to the worker- it actually de-values them.

How does a young person survive the camp culture where the work is never complete; your boss (the board) often is non-present on the site; and you are alone or with a smaller staff? The daily rewards of praise while working is non-existent. So often times, we sludge through our work, doing the best we can, but not knowing if it truly is good enough.

I could tell you to suck it up; grow up; get real; or just offer you a quick kick in the pants: I said I could, but I won't– not just yet.

For old timers, we are probably labeled, "thick skinned or even dinosaur skinned." It appears that we can get through years and years of toil and work and all done with little praise. At times this is true– we are an independent bunch that grew up without the "good job" mantra from our parents: we were told to mow the yard and that it should be done by supper. If it was not completed when dad came home, we ended up mowing through the supper hour– we were expected to carry our end of the load regardless of our age. For us, camp work comes naturally; we were born that way!

Younger staff grew up differently; they had few responsibilities thrust upon them from their parents. As a matter fact– the parents went out of their way to ensure there were no extra road blocks or interferences that kept their children from being fulfilled and happy with activities and praise. You blew your nose, Mom said, "Good Job!" You got yourself dressed, Mom praised you again. You ate your breakfast, "Aren't you a special child!" You have all heard it and I have seen it.

Mom didn't come to camp with you though. You are forced to start your day on the run with summer staff meetings, breakfast, chapels, activity schedules, lunch, activities, supper, evening chapel, camp fires– maybe you get to bed by 10 p.m., maybe not. And... you get up the next morning and do it all again. Your days are filled with: solving problems, intervening in crises, and directing staff around you. When your head hits the pillow you have gone through your day without a word of praise. It can suck the life out of a young person.

It is during those days that the goats get sorted from the sheep; it is during this time that those who are working at camp for a job and those who were called, get sorted out– one hangs in there and the other leaves discouraged and worn out.

Many of the old-timers in camp did not survive the brutal schedule by looking only at the summer or a busy fall retreat schedule. Many have survived and thrived by looking at the end. Like the farmer whose eyes are fixed on a landmark as he plows his fields, the seasoned camp director too sees all the way across a field, so that their plowing furrows remain straight, on course, without wavering or back tracking. They have stayed on track by keeping their eyes focused on the final results– being the instruments of spiritual growth to those they serve. *That is their calling.* That is their reward. That beats the shallow words of a doting mother.

In the end, I don't want a "Good Job." I want, *"Well done, good and faithful servant; thou hast been faithful over a few things, I will make you ruler over many things: enter thou into the joy of thy Lord."*

So in reality, I am telling you, "Suck it up!" I am telling you to "Quit looking at the mirror and start looking out the window!" I am telling you, "Let's roll! For the harvest truly is great... but **great** workers for the kingdom are few!"

## *Points to Ponder*

1. Where am I getting the strokes I need to get through a tough summer schedule?

2. What am I doing to encourage others around me to keep the course?

3. Do I have my mind set on the distant future, or am I only looking at next week?

4. Who can I find that will come alongside of me during my busiest days and encourage me to "press on?"

5. How can I reword my praise to others so that I am praising actual accomplishments and not praising for breathing or showing up?

*Yet those who wait for the LORD*
*will gain new strength;*
*they will mount up with wings like eagles,*
*they will run and not get tired,*
*they will walk and not become weary.*

*Isaiah 40:31*

# CHAPTER 28
## You are Sending a Message

Keep your signage up and your messages down. Have great directional signs around camp. But quit allowing the writing of stupid messages in your restrooms. Signs must be approved by the office... a 16-year-old should not be responsible for dictating part of the culture of camp.

Let me give you some examples that I have ripped off the walls of our restrooms during the summer while our Timothy Team students clean: "Please don't wash your feet in this toilet." "Flush stupid- the next person doesn't want to see any part of you." How about this one: "Use this paper towel— and hit the waste basket when you are done— I am not your mother!" Or above the urinal— "Out of order- go find a tree to pee on,"— complete with accurate anatomical drawings, and "if you sprinkle, when you tinkle, be a sweetie, and wipe the seatie," and finally, "We aim to please, you aim too, please"— complete with a happy face. Oh brother!

Messages written quickly and posted at random mean something. Unexpected guests arrive, use the bathroom, and see clever and sometimes very stupid wording haphazardly stuck to bathroom stalls, mirrors, or showers. Out of order is enough— additional information shared is usually too much. Not: "Out of order— kid just barfed on floor you might slip and fall into toilet!" This might be over the top.

It makes good fodder to laugh about around the staff table, but not all guests have your sense of humor!

Just one more sign found on the kitchen door: "Don't come in the kitchen— cook is throwing up and we don't want you to catch anything!"

We laugh about some of the innocent signs posted around our camp buildings by our younger staff and volunteers. However, many of us are just as guilty when we write and post newsletters on our websites. We do communicate the camp's culture and people do read what you allow to be placed on your websites. I can pretty well tell what type of culture a camp has by reading newsletters posted on their website: some are great... and some are not so great.

When you post certain letters, newsletters, announcement on your website... I am going to read it... and it better be good, positive and truly depict the REAL culture and vision of the camp. I don't want to be reading between the lines that someone has an ax to grind with life and the donor base. Donors do not want to hear desperate voices depicting their camp as just one flush away from the drain. Donors give when there is a vision that is clear and a ministry that knows where it is going and how it is going to get there.

I read many newsletters on websites that should not have ever left the office. Letters which should have been titled

"Woe is me... We are Job!" You may feel like it, the camp may be in that position– just never communicate that outside of your office walls. No one will give aid to a ship with only its mast flag out of the water– donors give when the boat is floating and moving ahead.

I never publicly talk about the problems of camp, I only write and talk about the opportunities at camp. I don't want people to read about backed up sewers, broken beds, or unpaid bills– I want to share the great testimonies of the cabin of seventh grade girls who all accepted Christ on Wednesday night. I want to let the testimony touch and stir the heart of a donor– that is the positive message that we need to proclaim and post on Facebook and on our websites.

I can't help it... here is my last sign I ripped off a vacuum, "Use this vacuum at your own risk!"

## *Points to Ponder*

1. What is our policy about signs posted by staff and volunteers?

2. What signs are we posting on Facebook and on our website?

3. Do we present ourselves like Job, "Woe is me" or like Paul, "I can do all things through Christ which strengthens me?"

4. Do we need to have someone check our attitude in every piece of literature that we produce and post?

5. Who repairs our vacuums and where do we put our "risky" vacuums?

*Immediately the fingers of a human hand
appeared and wrote on the plaster
of the wall of the king's palace,
opposite the lamp stand.*

*And the king saw the hand as it wrote.
Then the king's color changed, and his thoughts
alarmed him; his limbs gave way,
and his knees knocked together.*

*Daniel 5:5*

*(A very loose interpretation by me)*

## CHAPTER 29

# An Enigma— Youth Pastors

I fought them at first. Philosophically, coming from a home school perspective, I didn't see any need for a church to hire a 23 year old to instruct, educate, entertain, or counsel my children or anybody else's children. I reasoned, "That is what parents were made for!" I voiced it loudly and as often as I could get up on my soap box. When you're 33, you have not raised teen-agers yet; all one knows is the pliable, sponge-like four-year-olds who sit on your lap and listen to the same story about Bambi and Thumper for five times each evening. I have another opinion today.

Like it or not, youth pastors carry a lot of clout in the church. Seldom are they up front preaching, but they are back in the youth room, where they are spending a lot of the churches' money planning their program schedule for the year. Their positions are at stake if they anger too many parents by not providing enough "wholesome" activities for their children. So the calendar fills up with sleep-overs in the church sanctuary, trips to ball games, water park time is scheduled for the summer, skiing trips are put together for winter, and the district high school annual conference is penciled in as well.

"Oh and by the way... the camp up the road has a nice program, but since I didn't attend there as a child, I have no emotional attachment to it— but it is there if you want to fit it in between our youth group's schedule. Go ahead and try. And I don't want any of **my** key leadership people to go off working at camp all summer long either. I need them here!" exclaims the emphatic and overzealous youth pastor.

The enigma: How do you win over the new youth pastor who attended Lake Anne in Michigan as a child, but now leads a group of 60 in central Iowa? The answer: one kid at a time.

Rarely is the lifespan of a youth pastor at one church over 10 years. If I had to guess, I would say the average is more like three years or less. Either he does extremely well in his youth pastor's job and is offered an attractive job in a larger church, or the church moves him up to an assistant role as family ministries director or perhaps the associate pastor of counseling, or he just quits and gets a regular job. We all understand— the life of a youth pastor is demanding, unpredictable, family encroaching and parent driven. It can wear on a guy and sometimes moving on, up, or out is the best solution.

I can wait. I am content getting the churches' nine-year-old as a summer camper. The camp can give her such a wonderful experience that she comes back and attends some specialty type camps in Jr. High. Then we hire her as the dishwasher. Move her up to Jr. Counselor when she reaches eleventh grade— grooming her to take on the role as Sr. Counselor. I have bypassed the youth pastor. I haven't waited anxiously hoping that he will anoint our camp with his blessing and send HIS kids to our camp.

Then the snowball effect begins to take place. A high school staff member arrives home transformed and built up in her faith to such a high degree after spending the summer at camp; people notice. The church people begin to put the dots together and see that the metamorphosis of this young person happened while working at camp. They see and hear her passion for the lost. They see her integrity grow stronger and more evident in her decisions making. They see that she is the one whom others come to for advice and counsel. She has become the leader.

The parents pay attention too. They put the dots together too, and then they begin to insist that others attend camp and reap the rewards of a summer of spiritual growth and maturation. Pressure is applied to youth pastors by parents.

Yep ... I can wait... but I just have to stick around longer than the youth pastor.

## *Points to Ponder*

1. Do we have youth pastors who think their kids belong to them?

2. How do we help educate new youth pastors about our ministry?

3. How can the camp provide opportunities for youth pastors to come and see what we do during summer camp?

4. How would we describe our relationship with our youth pastors?

5. How can the camp encourage our youth pastors to press on when times get tough?

*Be patient, therefore, brethren,*
*until the coming of the Lord.*
*Behold, the farmer waits for the precious produce*
*of the soil, being patient about it,*
*until it gets the early and late rains.*

*You too be patient; strengthen your hearts,*
*for the coming of the Lord is at hand.*

*James 5:7-8*

# CHAPTER 30
# The Ugly Sister Syndrome

I was 16 once. I dated at one time. I dated with buddies too— they were called double dates. We dated sisters occasionally. One was cute, perky, and usually blond. The other, we'll just call her— physically challenged: plain, drab, dishwater blond— maybe a bit pudgy around the middle or with a crooked nose or teeth. I usually got the ugly one. I am not complaining— she usually was the most attentive, most appreciative, the most inclined to accept a second invitation. All in all, it wasn't horrible; it just wasn't exactly how I saw myself. I had higher expectations of the look of the girl I was going to spend $1.25 on for a movie and $1.50 for the pizza. I probably imagined a good-night kiss out of the whole transaction as well. Pizza, movie, kiss–a date-$2.75. I didn't get talked into double dating too often; I knew the Ugly Sister Syndrome— USS for short.

Fast forward 42 years: I have a wife of 36 years, 4 children, and 12 grandchildren. I shouldn't be thinking of dating. Especially double dating. But I do quite often. I do quite often when I visit older camps and see USS written all over the master plan. Ugly, plain buildings set next to new, more modern facilities. From this day forward, you can refer to your 1947 structure affectionately as "your ugly sister" instead of its proper name. Because, in reality, that is what it has become next to the building built in 1991 or 2012.

Let's continue with the dating analogy: No one wants to take her out either. No one wants to stay there. She is the last choice when the prom is just three days away. It is the hold-your-nose-building for three days until I get home. It is the bad bed, mold and mildew infested bathroom building, complete with torn carpet, cement floors and the personality of a toad- it just sits there! BLAH!

You are stuck with it. Remember the Millies in your churches; they are alive and ready to pounce on you if ever the word demolition is heard. But you know it, and the guests know it: this building is no longer an asset; it has grown into a liability. Millie just doesn't know it.

We had an "ugly sister" too in our main lodge. She wasn't 65 years old— complete with wrinkles and sun-spots. She was getting on 25 years old, complete with original furnaces, cement floors, stained carpet, and just okay bathrooms without the mildew. She was functionally awkward and clumsy for the amount of guests we now serve.

Three years later, we have installed 14 ton of ceramic tile, 7500 square feet of industrial carpet squares, buckets of paint, new siding, new roof, and a trailer full of new furniture. We have used enough make-up that now the ugly sister ain't looking so bad. In fact, she is taken out quite regularly these days.

Our 14,000 square foot building appeared to us as big as a mountain we needed to climb, as we looked at its sagging beds and worn through carpet. But, we started taking little steps at a time. One winter we installed the floor tile. The next winter we tackled the upstairs bathrooms. The next winter, we tore into the downstairs bathrooms. Step by step, piece by piece we re-imagined the original function of the building. And guess what? It will continue to get older and will be in need of more make-up— by next year there will be crow's lines that will need a little Botox injection to smooth it out and make it look pretty again!

So how does that help you restore the 1947 vintage building that is located in the wrong place? How can I gain any victories with it? How can I bring it up to our current standards? I can tell you one thing, you won't want to put a bag over her head— ugly is as ugly is.

Start with the little things. I can't tell you how many older camps I have visited that have piles and piles of program equipment, broken chairs, lamps that don't work, over-head projectors that are not used any more laying around in the most visual areas— the dining room and the chapel building.

Begin tossing. This doesn't cost anything. Hold a giant garage sale; bring out the neighborhood; sell hot dogs and chips and generate enough ready cash to buy paint and new light fixtures. Clean out all your closets and sheds and sell the extra stuff too!

If you begin to make this sweat investment into the building, a donor will come along and see you are still using outdated pews or rusty folding chairs and will comment,

"Your chapel looks nice, but gosh, you need new chairs. How much would it cost to replace them?" You better know the answer too! "$59.00 a chair from the Bertolini chair company," you should have on your tongue, "Delivered to the door. Would you like to see a picture of the tan colored ones I think you might like?"

This is where the resolve comes in to play. Look the problem in the eye; identify it as a problem; and then tackle it and FIX it. Quit blaming the economy, the board, and the guests. FIX IT! NOW!

I recently visited Camp Arrowhead near Glen Rose, Texas. Joe and Janet, with the help of a few volunteers have completely renovated over 20 buildings from this 1940's camp– in six years. This faithful couple took a worn out, tired looking facility and, with purpose and determination, transformed every building into a great facility. And they are in their 60's! If Joe and Janet can... so can you!

Your ugly sister can look pretty; you have to make her lose some weight (junk), put on some make-up (paint) and get some new high heels (flooring). But it has to be *your* resolve, *your* determination to have victory over this ugly building and turn it into a possible swan-like structure. Fairy tales still come true, but not without massive amounts of sweat, toil, vision and resolve. Never give up!

## Points to Ponder

1. What are five things we can do to our ugliest building to give it a face lift?

2. What will be the cost?

3. Who will do the work?

4. Is there a different purpose for this building other than how we are currently using it?

5. Where can I find some cheap paint, carpet, and light fixtures?


*....Whatever you do, do it all for the glory of God.*
*I Corinthians 10:31*

## CHAPTER 31
# All Hat, No Cattle!

B ad beds, bad food equals mad guests. I touched on it earlier. Those who are involved in guest services and hospitality in the secular world "get it!" They get it so well you can move around from Motel 6 to Ritz Carlton to Carnival Lines to Disney World and feel that they ALL get it- all with a different twist, but all with care, quality, and taste for the level of service you would expect to pay. You expect 20-dollar-service for your 20 bucks. You expect 100-dollar-care for your hard earned 100 bucks. Your expectation level has been met– which makes you feel like you at least won.

Here is where some camps don't "get it." They miss the mark! They are over-priced and under-delivered. What do I mean? I mean, you are charging $9 for a $5 meal. Struggling camps are most vulnerable to slip into this mindset. They need extra cash now, and they think the quickest way to get the cash is to raise the price to a level that they think can generate the needed cash. What actually happens is: indeed they win for one weekend with the booking of the retreat, but they lose when it comes to repeat business.

Think about yourself. Where do you continually take your family out to eat? I know where I go. I go to Hickory Park in Ames; my wife and I can both eat for $13.50. Both of us will be full, satisfied with the quality of the food and leave smiling and content; I purposely schedule my trips to Lowes for supplies so that I can dine at Hickory Park– every time I can.

On the other hand, I stopped into a little, quaint café in Macon, Missouri one time, hoping to find a home-cooked breakfast. What I received was a plate full of grease-soaked eggs, toast smothered with old butter and smashed down from the buttering process, and with the only bathroom conveniently located within hearing distance of my table! And I was charged $8.00 for the plate of greasiness. Not only would I not stop there again, I am telling you not to stop there, and I will continue to tell others not to stop there.

Unfulfilled expectations: Match the price to the quality of the experience and you will always have repeat guests.

Don't oversell. Your tour guide gets carried away when she give tours to potential guest groups. Words like marvelous, awesome, fantastic, and unbelievable, pontificate from the mouth of the guide, but in reality they can only deliver okay, good enough, and not bad results. John Wooden, the most winning coach in NCAA basketball at UCLA used to tell his players, "Don't tell me what you can do; show me what you can do." I think if that philosophy was good enough for the 10 time NCAA national champion coach Wooden, it should be good enough for us in the camping business.

I always want the retreat guests to smile and say, "*WOW,* *WOW,* and *WOW!*" Over produce and under promise; your guests will return over and over and over again.

## *Points to Ponder*

1. Do we oversell our services? Is our food really that good?

2. In town, would I pay $9 for a meal like what we serve?

3. What would it take to WOW our guests with our food and service?

4. When we give tours to potential guests, are we realistic in what we say we can deliver?

5. What five things can we change on our menu that will WOW our guests?


*And whatsoever ye do, do it heartily,*
*as to the Lord, and not unto men.*

*Colossians 3:23*

## CHAPTER 32

# Hyperseeing...

When Gutzon Borglum's housekeeper first saw Mount Rushmore, she asked the sculptor, "Mr. Borglum, how did you know Mr. Lincoln was in that rock?" Her innocent question explains hyperseeing: an artist's ability to look at a rough piece of stone and see it in its final perfected form.

When I read this, I thought– that is what I can do– I can hypersee. I love to look at a piece of ground with some buildings on it and see a great camp being resurrected or resuscitated back into a vibrant and active facility. I love to see old buildings and imagine them being transformed into something useful and beautiful.

Could I hypersee what our camp was going to be when I first started? Not in a thousand years; I might have seen parts of it, but I never knew it would look like Lincoln. I just knew enough that if I were persistent enough, dedicated enough, creative enough, something good was going to happen.

Where are you today with your camp? I have talked to many directors over the years and many of them are not seeing anything: there is little understanding of what their camp could become. They are caught up in the here and now of survival. Survival is not a healthy position to be in: systems shut down to preserve resources; there is no thought about a year in advance, there is only thought about tomorrow. It becomes almost impossible to visualize a Lincoln from a mass of old buildings, old systems, uncommitted churches and low attendance.

If you can't see the full 3-D face of Lincoln, can you at least see his nose, one eye or his beard? When faced with years and years of deferred maintenance, the job does appear overwhelming. There needs to be a point of entry; a place to begin.

Sometimes we just have to show up; show up and get started on a building; show up and clean out a room; show up and start throwing and tossing; just show up dressed in work clothes and wearing gloves and goggles.

Todd and his wife showed up at His Thousand Hills Camp in Pennsylvania nine years ago. The camp was in need of revitalizing; for years the camp had not invested in routine maintenance or upkeeps. Todd and his wife rolled up their sleeves. Todd states, "When we arrived, the camp had a history of no money and no repairs. We have been here for nine years without any salary and we have done nothing but paint, clean and fix since we arrived. Eventually we received $200,000 in two gifts, and even that money went to capital improvements. We stretched those dollars further than any dollar has been stretched before. I have a desire to build new structures, but I knew I needed to update the old."

History can do two things: work for you or work against you. When history works for you, it is called *traditions*. It is the bell tower next to the dining room where all the staff meets and entertains campers prior to every meal. It is the special cooking area next to the lake where trail break-fasts have been lovingly prepared for the past 40 years by staff who care for their guests and pay close attention to all the details of the shore-line breakfast: never forgetting the special type of syrup that has been used for 30 straight years and poured over pancakes made from the same reci-pe and cooked over the same 48" by 48" homemade griddle that the founder of the camp made in 1952. That is history working for you.

You know what it feels like when history works against you. It feels like you are suffocating under a huge load. History can be the enemy and can sit heavy on your chest.

Whatever the history, whatever you are dealt to manage, it can be turned around. It can be re-imagined into something sustainable and vibrant. Ministry can be restored; lives can be touched by the Spirit of God around the same campfire circle rings located in the same spot as 60 years ago.

Let me lay out some hope for you. Here are some steps that you, the director, and your board will need to address soon-er than later. If you are reading this hoping for answers, you are probably desperate or at least stalled. This is not a book for successful, thriving camps that are adding on and grow-ing because of steady and strong leadership. This is for you who are tired and weary and need some answers... quick!

There comes a time in a camp's history when the board and staff need to buckle down and take care of what they have on the grounds. There needs to be a major shift in the minds of the staff; they have to change from wanting something new to a mindset of how do we update and re-configure the old? It is much easier to try to buy yourself out of the hole than to dig yourself out of the hole through hard work.

As a visionary leader, it is easy for me to walk into a camp and re-invent and reorganize the buildings and the program. I can hypersee what could be in the future. I can see that there is possible life and opportunities, but I cannot make the leadership of the camp roll up their sleeves and just show up every day to tackle one building or one closet; *their minds need to change before their hearts can feel hope.*

Can I see into another camp's future and tell you what it might look like in 10 years? I could, but in reality, you have to be the one who becomes steadfast and focused on accomplishing something good every day towards the end product.

Now get your gloves on and go to work! Do it every day!

## Points to Ponder

1. Can we see the camp that could be in the stone called "our older buildings?"

2. How do we help the staff to see "what could be" instead of what is?

3. Does our staff have the "can do" attitude that will help us transform the camp?

4. How do we train our staff to understand the word "resolve?"

5. Do we look at other camps and "wish," or do we look at other camps and say, "We can do that!"

*In the last days, God says,*
*I will pour out my Spirit on all people.*
*Your sons and daughters will prophesy,*
*your young men will see visions,*
*your old men will dream dreams.*

*Acts 2:17*

CHAPTER 33

# The Trust Factor—
# Advice for the New Director

O ne of the most important aspects of starting fresh at a camp; your trust meter is set at zero. That means you have no history with the organization as to how you accomplish your work. Guests and donors do not know if you can accomplish the work assigned to you. They have yet to hear you declare the first project you hope to accomplish.

Protect your trust meter and make sure you have some major victories that back up your words. Broken trust will saddle you with a tax! Stephen M.R. Covey in his book, *The Speed of Trust,* says this about building trust or the lack of trust: "It will either be a tax that will cost a person time and money, or it will be a dividend that will add speed and lower the cost of execution of responsibilities."

I recently visited a camp that has been struggling for the last 10 years. The camp has gone through three directors in ten years, which in turn has dried up funds and participation by formerly loyal churches. What happened? With every new director, new promises and new vision were presented to donors and guest groups– however, as the directors suddenly left, the donors and guest groups were thrown into confusion. They no longer understood where the camp was headed with their programs or the development of their facilities.

In the case mentioned above, it was not necessarily each new camp director's fault that the donor/guest groups were confused. It actually started back with the board and the lack of clear direction defined by the board. These last three directors were following a director who had been at the camp for 12 years; the board had relied on this long-term director to create and implement the vision and direction of the camp. The board made the assumption the new directors would understand and follow with a similar vision.

Take-a-way: Have a clear understanding where the board wishes the new director to take the camp. In the interview process or at least in the first three board meetings, the new director has to have clarification regarding past direction and how the board sees the past influencing the future direction under the new director's leadership. Today, the latest director at this camp is truly paying a tax. It is costing him more time and money to convince donors to begin giving again. Guest groups who used the camp faithfully for years have opted out and placed their loyalty in other camps.

First, you must admit the problem– *lack of trust*. You have to understand that it is your main problem. It is the problem causing your problems. Your problems are not your problem; lack of trust is your problem. Get to the root of it.

How can the new director regain trust? It can be regained.

Here is what you need to do ASAP: you must have some small, quick victories. Don't make large, complicated promises that will take months to raise money and implement. Begin small with very do-able projects that can be accomplished in one week or less. Pick particular projects carefully. I would always pick projects that are the most visible to the guest or donors. Tackle one room at a time with new paint, refurbishing furniture, or replacing carpet.

Work on restoring trust one bite at a time; broken trust is the elephant in the room that nobody wants to talk about; eat him one bite at a time. And then keep talking about the next bite, and then the next bite. Stop talking about the entire huge elephant. It is over-whelming if you try to restore trust with one big swoosh of action.

Professional advice: Southwest Airlines founder, Herb Helleher, stated when asked what his strategic plan was, "It is called doing things!"

Now go and do something! And be quick about it!

## *Points to Ponder*

1. Is there a lack of trust by our guest groups and donors?

2. What caused this lack of trust?

3. What is our strategic plan?

4. What project can we begin with to make the loudest statement?

5. When do we begin?

*Whoever can be trusted with very little*
*can also be trusted with much,*
*and whoever is dishonest with very little*
*will also be dishonest with much.*

*Luke 16:10*

## CHAPTER 34
# The Intern: Cream Rises to the Top...

**T**itles don't matter much to me; I am old enough not to care. Call me anything you want; just don't call me late for lunch.

Young staff feels differently; they like the title. They think it defines them as a person, so I oblige. I give them a title that actually describes what they do; it also implies the thing I want them to major on. It becomes their driving force— the top line on their job description.

I didn't like my title of Executive Director. It sounded like a position of high authority— so I changed it to what I think I really do— Director of Vision and Design. I spend most of my day thinking about the future and designing buildings and systems; the title accurately describes my work.

We have had three interns work for us for a couple years. Each has had a primary role, either construction or guest services. When we promoted them to a full-time position, we ordered a professionally made name tag with their new position title. I intentionally gave them a title that would be accurate only about 15% of their time, but it was a title that I wanted them to grow towards. Serena and Melia are now Hospitality Coordinators. Tony is the Media Technician.

Over the time they have worked for us, we have identified where their sweet spots are and we gave a title to fit that gift; they still are doing housekeeping, food service and construction, but their title identifies them to the role they like best and where they are best suited.

I love to empower staff to the things they are best wired to do. Tony can help in construction projects, but he excels at running the sound systems. Serena and Melia can clean rooms, but they love to do extra special things for our guests to make the guests feel cared for and loved.

Internships at camp are priceless. If a young person has a desire to serve and a desire to develop his skills, camp is a perfect place available to the 20-something student. They are given enormous opportunities to locate and develop their sweet spot without spending one dollar on college tuition.

In exchange, the camp gets inexpensive labor without paying out benefits and vacation time. Interns allow the camp to fill the holes without bringing on a full time staff member. We use our internship program as a training ground and a polishing time to bring along a young person prior to the camp putting them on full-time staff. Internships can be the first leg of a leadership program; the intern first learns who and what they are. Then they are capable of leading.

For me, I love to watch interns for a few months and try to see where an intern excels. I want to empower them with even more responsibilities where they can use their gifts. Sometimes it is a hit and miss proposition, and other times their gifts rise to the top immediately: cream always rises to the top.

In many ways, the stunted camp is similar to the intern when he first arrives at camp: the stunted camp does not know who it is, what it does best or where or how it will end up.

I pray that reading this book will help clarify you as a camp and move you forward into becoming the camp you are capable of becoming.

## *Points to Ponder*

1. How do we utilize our interns?

2. Do we see the interns as cheap labor or do we see them as potentially full-time staff-in-training?

3. What are our objectives for our internship program?

4. Is there anybody in whom we have invested a year into that would make a great full-time staff?

5. Why don't our titles depict actual responsibilities?

6. Are we a stunted camp because we are not utilizing our God-given talents and passions correctly? Explain how we became stunted.

*Train up a child in the way he should go;*
*even when he is old he will not depart from it.*

*Proverbs 22:6*

# CHAPTER 35
# 49/51 Rule

I love the concept lived out by Danny Meyer, author and restaurateur as he breaks down his guest experiences in his many New York City restaurants.

Meyers writes, "Every guest wants their expectations met... they want their food hot, to taste good, a clean restaurant, friendly and timely staff— that's the 49%; but if they only get that part— they leave without feeling cared for, feeling needed or appreciated, feeling important, or feeling that we were on their side. It is the feeling side that brings back guests— that is the 51%."

Repeat it often, then repeat it again, "It is such a pleasure to serve you."

I started in the camping business in 1979; I knew nothing. I had attended camp for a few years when I was 10 to 12 years old. I fell into camping by accident; I thought I was going to be a college professor. I took the job as a camp ranger for a nearby Girl Scout camp after finishing graduate school.

I did not receive any instructions on how to do my job other than to have the buildings ready for the weekend scout troops; I cleaned, I mowed the grass, and I had fire wood cut for them. I provided no food service for these weekend retreats. I would stop down to their lodge once I saw the cars arrive at camp on Friday evenings and would make myself available to meet their needs.

Not only was I untrained, I was actually not a great fit to be the ranger: I did not like grease and I did not really know much about the mechanical side of being the camp caretaker. I loved to mow and paint and make things look nice, but I could not repair a motor if my life depended on it. Former camp rangers were more mechanical than I was.

Regardless of my lack of a mechanical skill set, I excelled at my job— at least according to the troop leaders. And the troop leaders talked. They talked back to the main office in Des Moines which wrote me my paycheck. They gave me great reviews as the new camp ranger. Was it because I had the technical skills to make the camp run smoother? No! It was because I majored on the 51% stuff: I showed I cared.

In 1985 I moved to Hidden Acres. I began as the Property Manager. I was also the weekend retreat host. But now our weekends became more complicated– we offered food service.

I began to host our first retreats in a new lodge. The building's paint was barely dry before our first retreat arrived. I had never managed a retreat; never been to one; didn't know what to expect or how I should really act. The lodge was all self-contained, with a dining and kitchen area, a meeting room, a gym, and 15 sleeping rooms upstairs–

enough for 80— all bunk beds. It was new. It was nice. It was state-of-the-art for 1985.

At the same time, the camp had very few program areas: no lake, no climbing wall, no horses. There were walking paths. There was a half-sized gym for guest groups to play in.

So instead of moaning and groaning about all the camp did not have, I set out to give extra value to our weekend guests; I loved on them. I showed that I really cared for them. I met their needs over and above what they expected: they returned the next year, and the next year.

We grew. We added a lake. We brought in horses. We built a climbing wall, zip line, and a giant swing. But we never stopped handing out the soft stuff: the love and care.

Every staff member knows that Friday after lunch is P to P time. We shift gears from our Projects of the week to our People of the weekend. It is a mental shift more than a physical shift. Each staff member knows to be on the look-out and to make himself available to any retreater as the cars begin to trickle into camp on a Friday afternoon. Projects continue, but not with the same intensity as Monday through Friday noon. People become our priority.

We also remind the staff of the eight foot rule: If a guest comes within eight feet of you; you had better be looking into their eyes and smiling along with greeting them.

This is my challenge to you. Perhaps your buildings have some deficiencies. Perhaps you don't have much in program areas for your guest groups to enjoy while they are at your camp. But you do have a heart. You do have two hands to serve. You do have time to wait and serve your guests.

You do have the ability to concentrate on the 51% stuff– the soft stuff of life.

You could have the nicest, cleanest buildings, but if your staff is preoccupied and non-attentive to the guest groups– you will have guest groups that will leave your camp on Sunday with just an *okay* feeling about their camp experience. When you lavish love and care on your guest groups, you will get emails back from group coordinators that state they "felt loved and cared for by the camp staff."

You can't buy that type of marketing. Love and care beats any marketing program offered up in a box: Love and care trumps hype and horn blowing every day of the week. If you feel your marketing program is subpar due to the lack of time and knowhow– know that love and care will go much further than a four-colored brochure, a church visit, or any social media hype.

Well-cared-for retreaters will become your marketing agents for you. So relax... you CAN become a marketing expert: it is called "the love and care" department of the camp.

Now go and hug someone!

## Points to Ponder

1. How can we begin our new marketing program this weekend?

2. How do we "retrain" our staff to move from their projects to the people?

3. Does all of our staff know the eight foot rule?

4. Are we getting emails back from our guests about the care and love they received from the staff? If not, why not?

5. How do we start a P to P program?

*Let each of you look not only to your own interests,*
*but also to the interests of others.*

*Philippians 2:4*

# CHAPTER 36
## Part of the Community

D on't forget your Judea; your village or town near the camp. They too need to see your testimony lived out in front of them.

The un-churched community that surrounds the camp looks suspiciously at the camp: "Is it a cult that is hanging out in the woods outside of town; another Jamestown; a commune?" The town wonders.

Coffee shop talk is abundant. If the camp does not define itself to the community, the community will define the camp around the local coffee shop tables. Speculation and rumors run rampant.

We work hard at protecting our reputation. Do we advertise in the local newspaper? No. Are we a local school district sports team supporter? No. Are we members of Rotary or Kiwanis? No. We don't do any of these things.

Instead, we invite the town out to camp! A picture is worth a thousand words. We get the local community out to camp to rub shoulders with our staff. We want them to see our facilities. We invite them to use our facilities. We are generous back to the community.

The local wrestling team has their year-end awards banquet at camp. We provide the local fire and rescue squad with their annual fund-raising supper– all free to them and our staff acts as the host and we promote the event for them. The local schools use our gym for basketball practice for the fifth and sixth graders. We open our indoor pool to the community of older ladies who need to exercise three times a week throughout the winter. We open up our inn for neighbors to use if out-of-town guests need a bed.

What have we done by opening up the camp to a secular population? We have given many people their first look at what the church should look like: hospitable and loving. When our local school teachers come to camp for an in-service training day– teachers are wary and cautious to love and care; you can sense it in their body language that warmness and thoughtfulness are not part of their normal work place culture.

We control the coffee shop talk– we give out so much love and care, even old, unsaved men can't gossip about us! Instead, they become our cheerleaders too!

## Points to Ponder

1. What does our community think about our camp?

2. What can we do to show our community that we are a healthy organization that is community minded?

3. What are the things available at camp that we could offer to the local school district?

4. How are we controlling the "coffee shop gossip" or does it define the camp?

5. How can we prepare for the influx of non-churched guest groups?

*Keep your conduct among the Gentiles honorable,
so that when they speak against you as evildoers,
they may see your good deeds
and glorify God on the day of visitation.*

*I Peter 2:12*

# CHAPTER 37
# Form Follows Function

I have seen some crazy looking camp buildings. I have seen big buildings with no bathrooms. I have seen buildings with gabled roofs that slope down onto a center flat roof. I have seen narrow hallways and stairs. I have seen buildings with no inside stairs. These buildings were designed by professional architects.

I like architects; I just won't hire one. They are nice people; I just don't want to use their services. I want to do it by myself!

Here is why I choose not to involve an architect in any of our design work:

- An architect costs money! Lots of money. I would rather buy boards than pay for his knowledge.

- An architect will add cost to the overall building by putting extras into the building that will give glory to him and his firm– extras are put into a building to enhance their reputation and not to enhance how the building will function.

- Sometimes the transfer from paper to reality leaves a lot to the imagination and the builders have to modify the original plans to fit reality.

Let me illustrate how an architect will design something into a building that ends up costing extra dollars. I gave a tour of our recreation building to another camp– their architect came along for ideas. When we looked at our gym, I emphatically stated, "Leave the high windows out of the room. There are more functions to the room when you can totally black out the room." Their architect was more worried about how it would look and insisted that the gym room should have the high windows.

I told the architect about our church sanctuary in town– with architect designed high windows in it– today the church is spending several thousand dollars trying to darken the windows so the sun won't shine in the preacher's face. Architects will put windows in places you cannot clean or maintain; they do it for pretty; I design it for practical.

We do all the design work ourselves. We start with scratch paper and pen. A general idea of the function of the building is written out. We discuss foyers, closets, kitchens, bathrooms, meeting spaces, activity areas, and bedrooms. We discuss the types of groups that will be using the new building. We will discuss how and where we want the traffic to flow. We discuss the types of materials that we will use in the building. We discuss flooring, lighting, doorways, and fireplaces.

We do not talk about what the building will look like: we establish the function first. Form always follows function.

All the functions of the building need to be written down before floor plans are drawn. Once function is determined, we are ready to draw up a floor plan. We start with general big room space, and work down to the smallest spaces. We know if the room is going to be used for tables and chairs, we adjust the size of the room accordingly: we like to provide about 15 square feet per person for dining space. If it is for a lecture type room, we provide about 10 square feet per person; this gives ample room for stage and aisles.

We love foyers on our buildings. Just look at an old church; foyers were non-existent; a few coat racks were the only amenities that older churches provided when you stepped into the building. If there are any additions added to these antiquated church buildings, it is usually a foyer with plenty of gathering space and bathrooms.

We don't want to have to remodel after a few years, so we build a foyer into every building: a large foyer. When you enter our family life center there is a 3000 square foot foyer. Is that excessive? No... just right. When crowds of 300 or more are at camp, we want them to be able to mingle in our foyer. We want to provide space for waiting, relaxing, and for coffee drinking and snacks. We want a fireplace and comfortable seating. We want a neutral place for guests to be able to come for early morning coffee, or late night fun and games. We are currently designing a 20,000 square foot dining room and kitchen: we will have a 2000 square foot foyer for guests to wait and queue up for their meal time, complete with bathrooms, fireplace and a soft chair sitting area.

When we design buildings, we make sure access to a bathroom is convenient and assessable to all of our guests. Our staff returned home from a CCCA meeting a few years ago and commented, "We had to leave the dining room building and go outside to find a bathroom!" All I could say was, "Poor planning and a poor architect!" Bathrooms need to be within a short distance from the front door.

When we build two-story buildings, we allow for stairs to be on the inside of the building. Outside stairs can work in summer, but they are brutal in Iowa winters. And our inside stairs are wide enough that two people can pass each other coming or going. Three foot stairways and hallways don't cut it. Five to six feet is best. Don't cheat on this. I have visited a camp with long three foot hallways– you have to turn sideways when passing a person walking the opposite direction.

We purposely design a kitchen in every lodge we build. Do we encourage groups to cook their own food? Not exactly; but without this kitchen, the lodge becomes limited. With a kitchen, we provide an opportunity for a youth group who is on a limited budget to have an inexpensive retreat– they bring their own cook and food. Most of their food is simple food, but a stove, refrigerator and sink is needed to even cook soup or hot dogs. We provide an outside gas grill.

We pay attention to bathroom design. We design showers with extra space for dressing and clothes. I recently looked over the floor plans for a new shower house for a camp in Wyoming, drawn up by an architect; he had a dressing room placed four feet across from the shower space– meaning a naked body would have to walk across the hallway to dress his self! No thanks! We utilize a cement counter top that is nearly indestructible by 16-year-olds sitting on it. We over-build, knowing that younger guests will under-think.

We have one staff person who controls the interior décor of all our buildings. She decides on color of tile. She decides on paint, curtains, and wall hangings. She coordinates all details that make a building home-like instead of a steril-ized commercial building.

We utilize HardiePlank siding; we have found this product holds paint indefinitely; we think it is nearly indestructible. We have utilized steel roofs. We use steel soffits and fascia. We try to eliminate outside maintenance. Cedar siding is pretty to look at and looks more "campy," but I have never heard a director with 10-year-old cedar siding being happy about the way it looks today; I know more who are ripping it off and replacing it with a cement board type of product.

I can hear you rolling your eyes now. You are saying, "I couldn't even build a decent dog house! How do you expect me to think about the details of what was just written?" You don't need to know how to build; you just need to know all the details of the function of the building.

You need to know how a potential guest group will move and retreat inside this building; architects will not be able to anticipate this like the director and his staff can. House-keepers and retreat hosts need to be involved. Ladies need to be involved. Maintenance staff need to be involved. Con-struction crews need to be involved. The décor staff must be involved.

When the entire staff works on planning the building: the closets will be in the correct place; the flooring will be easy to clean; the laundry room will be laid out correctly; the duct work will fit in the space provided; the windows will be easy to open and clean; the bathrooms will be functional and sturdy. You will have a building that will outlast you and will be functional for years to come.

Poorly planned buildings can be more of a hindrance than a blessing: just look at your buildings that were built 40 years ago! You need to look no further.

Go ahead and hire an architect if you must; they do know what they are doing. However, if you haven't done your homework and decided the function of the structure before the architect designs the form— you may end up with a building that does not meet your needs: pretty to look at— but it functions like ugly.

## Points to Ponder

1. How do we want our next building to function?

2. How can all the staff contribute to the design of our new building prior to meeting with an architect?

3. Who does pick the colors and the décor?

4. What are the deficiencies in our current buildings, and what do we want to do differently on the next camp structure?

5. Are we building something for our tastes, or for the comfort of our guests?

*According to the grace of God which was given to me, like a wise master builder I laid a foundation, and another is building on it.*

*But each man must be careful how he builds on it. For no man can lay a foundation other than the one which is laid, which is Jesus Christ.*

*Now if any man builds on the foundation with gold, silver, precious stones, wood, hay, straw, each man's work will become evident; for the day will show it because it is to be revealed with fire, and the fire itself will test the quality of each man's work.*

*If any man's work which he has built on it remains, he will receive a reward.*

*1 Corinthians 3:10-14*

# Chapter 38
# Good Enuf!

G ood enuf! That has been our camp motto! We have grown in stages... we didn't get gold plated the first round... but we kept increasing our quality within our buildings. When furniture wore out, we burned it and replaced it with something better. The Lord supplied our needs in the most unusual ways over the years.

We accept anything anybody will give us; sometimes it works out great, and sometimes it is a piece of junk. We take it and smile anyway.

- One of our churches decided they needed new church chairs... we got their rose colored padded chairs... were they the color we would have purchased? No, but they were in great shape and they were free... good enuf!

- We go to many restaurant auctions where we purchase many stainless steel work areas; do they match and fit perfectly? No, but we purchased them for 10 cents on the dollar compared to new. They worked good enuf!

- A restaurant went out of business and we purchased a van load of tablecloths and napkins. Were they perfect? No, but we paid $50 for everything. Good enuf!

- We have been a member of NAEIR since 1986. We have received: carpet, tile, windows, doors, paper, hardware, floor mats, pool tables, furniture, and ice melt by the truck load. Did it all match exactly? No, but it was near free and we put it to use in many of our buildings. It was good enuf!

- We purchased lounge furniture, area rugs, foosball tables, chairs, and desks from the defunct Pillsbury College in Owatonna, Minnesota. Was it exactly what we wanted? No, but it was good enuf!

- Iowa State University needed chairs removed from a building by 5 p.m. We loaded up 500 very orange chairs as quickly as we could and paid them $.05 each. Yep, for a nickel each we turned our dining room into a big orange pumpkin. Was it the color of our dreams? No, but it was good enuf to get us by for three or four years.

- I rented a truck and hauled 500 seats out of Veterans Auditorium storage area. We were using a 60' x 60' tent for our summer chapel. Were they pretty and padded? No... they were free... and were good enuf!

I am trying to tell you: it doesn't have to be perfect as long as it is better than it used to be. Eventually, things wear out and we replace it with something better; we try to upgrade each time.

We are frugal!

We are careful and watch how we spend the money that is entrusted to us. With our frugality, we have saved thousands of dollars that we have poured into constructing new buildings. We drove junky, donated pickups for years so that extra cash could buy boards and nails. We used what we had available and kept it as clean as possible. We sometimes couldn't make it perfect, but it was good enuf.

Today, it is easier to purchase new furniture and matching carpet. Today we can drive nicer trucks and vans. Today we can purchase new chairs and dining room tables.

But we got by with "good enuf" for a season, so that we could build up the business that gives us extra income today and into the future.

## *Points to Ponder*

1. Would we accept a $.05 orange chair to get us by for a season? When do we say no to free stuff?

2. Which of our staff is available and has the interest to attend auctions?

3. Where do we store excess supplies until needed?

4. How can the principle of being "frugal" be taught to the entire staff?

5. When is it okay not to just "get by?"

*Delight yourself in the Lord, and he will give you the desires of your heart.*

*Psalm 37:4*

## CHAPTER 39

# Transitioning Out—
# Replacing a Director!

There will come a time when you will be put out to pasture: retired. Your body and mind eventually slow down and someone younger with more energy and vigor will need to replace you. What have you done to prepare for the day? Who have you brought alongside you in your last eight years to take over the reins of the organization? How have you taught the entire staff to maintain the culture that you have faithfully developed over the past 20 or 30 years?

If you have not anticipated this, expect some rough waters after you are gone from camp; you will be setting up the next director for failure. The transition between long-time directors and the new director needs time to mature and settle into a natural rhythm.

I have watched camp after camp falter for years when the baton is passed poorly or not at all. The new director is plopped down into an established culture without ever learning or appreciating what has happened over the last

30 years. They are usually eager to prove themselves as the new leader and begin to change direction quickly.

When culture is changed too quickly, confusion reigns. When an established camp culture is thrown by the wayside by the younger, energetic leader, and replaced with something a bit more hip and edgy, you have problems with donors: old donors who like camp the way it used to be: *Conservative!* And, older donors can stop giving very quickly.

Guests and donors like the known. Guests feel comfortable with traditions. Donors love to trust the leader of the organization they are donating towards. Change either one of these elements too quickly, and there is doubt and lack of trust.

One of the best transitions I have seen has been at Camp Forest Springs, in Wisconsin. Dick Angelo has handed off the reigns of the directorship to Pat Petkau. Pat leads the day-to-day functions and staff of the camp. Dick kept his office and the position as ambassador and fund raiser. It is Dick's face that donors see on the banquet circuit. It is his face they trust. Pat is increasing in power and authority every year; and the donor base is slowly getting used to the new guy. The transition is seamless.

I could name countless transitions at camps that were not seamless. The director either left unexpectedly, had health issues, or was just fired. The camps become stunted for several years because of this poor transition.

If a camp board has a long-standing director to replace, the board needs to begin the process five to seven years out. The board needs to begin to adjust their way of thinking. They need to begin to identify the exact gifts of their long-term director; they may have been a great fund raiser, an administrator, or their gifts may have been in developing the physical elements of camp.

The camp board has to decide if they want to continue with the same gift set or if they think the age of the camp demands a different set of gifts. I always said that I was the developer of the camp I work in, but the next person who replaces me should be an administrator.

The board should at least look at any possible candidates already working for their organization. An inside promotion is the simplest to manage— the candidate already knows the culture, knows the churches, and knows the pastors who regularly attend the camp. He definitely has the inside track.

If no suitable candidate is available, the board and the long-standing director must begin the process of finding someone to whom this director would be willing to pass the baton on to. I believe it is very important that the director has a role in finding the next director. Nobody knows the camp like he does. Nobody understands what gifts will be needed to take over. Boards who exclude the director from this process are setting themselves up for heartache.

It is a slow process. The new director needs to be hired at least four years before the long-term director retires. The new director doesn't have to be given the entire job description; in their first year or two, only 50% of the eventual job description should be handed over. Piece by piece, responsibility by responsibility, the old director will release to the new director. Eventually, the old director's role becomes the ambassador and a fund raiser for the camp– until they finally remove themselves from the camp completely and move to Florida.

This is an extremely difficult time for the old director; they are handing over 30+ years of their life to someone new and unknown. However, if they don't perform this well, their 30 years spent at camp can come to a screeching halt very quickly. They have to swallow their pride and make the transition work smoothly in order to ensure there will be a future for the camp.

I have seen it in churches, in schools, and in camps. Done well you hardly notice the change. Done wrong, it creates open sores and wounds that fester and ache for years to come. I have seen organization fizzle and die from poor planning on the board's part. Don't do that to your camp. Don't suddenly decide to retire without investing time and energy into the next leader.

Begin the process sooner than later: begin it now!

## Points to Ponder

1. Has the new director been identified?

2. What steps are needed so that the retiring director can work with this new replacement and pass off responsibilities in a timely fashion?

3. Has the camp board prepared far enough in advance so that the transition is seamless?

4. Are there target dates set for transitioning certain responsibilities?

5. Which mower will the old guy get to use? Will there be a golf cart for him to get around in?

*For I am already being poured out as an offering,
and the time for me to depart is at hand.
I have competed well; I have finished the race;
I have kept the faith!
Finally the crown of righteousness is reserved for me.
The Lord, the righteous Judge, will award it to me in
that day— and not to me only,
but also to all who have set their affection
on his appearing.*
2 Timothy 4:6-8

# CHAPTER 40
## In Five Years—

**F**ive years can seem like an eternity when you are anxious to grow and become the camp you were made to be; five years goes by quickly for one who is near retirement.

So I ask again, "What do you want to become in five years? Do you have any sense of what you might look like if you would put your sweat equity into this organization called the camp?" I think I can see it... but the results are up to you.

Much of what you will need to do will boil down to how committed you are to making the camp into a growing and vibrant institution which has more good years ahead of it than behind it.

If you heard anything from reading this book, you heard the words resolve, determination, commitment, stubbornness, and sweat. You heard phrases like, "Yes, we can!" You heard, "It is a pleasure to serve you!" You heard, "Yep... we can do that!"

Much of the success in Christian camping is the attitude rather than the facilities or lack of money or the shortage of guests. When camp staff exudes friendliness and warmth– you will win. When camp staff are more concerned about their rules and their facilities– you will lose.

There does need to be an alignment between the director and the camp board. There does need to be a staff in place who is willing and capable of doing many things; regardless if the duty is on or off their normal job descriptions.

For those of you who are part of growing and fulfilled camps– you get it. You have nodded your head several times through these pages and understood my heart and my attitude. You "get it"! You know how to make things happen at camp so that guests want to come back for your love and care. Your camps are alive and well. This is true for all sizes: small, medium, large, and extra large.

If you are part of a stunted camp, you must hypersee your facility and programs and create a vision. Once the vision is created, you have to have the fortitude to execute your vision. The vision has to be director-driven and staff-implemented; the director has to be relentless; you have to be focused; you have to never give up.

If you are not going to stay at a camp for the long haul, you shouldn't have even applied; as a matter of fact, you will do more harm than good. Short-termers are not welcome.

During your first three years, don't expect to make too much forward progress; you can't gain your constituencies' *full* trust in three years. During the first three years, a director will only begin to understand the guest groups and the culture of the camp. You will only begin to become acquainted with donors and pastors.

Directors who stay longer can begin to influence future successes. At five years, you can leave your fingerprints around camp that others can identify. People will remember you positively and can point out accomplishments made during your time.

At 10 years a director's footprints will be evident. You will have influenced a group of children through their entire school years. You should have built a couple buildings.

At 20 years you will have left butt-drag marks that create a path for others to follow. After 20 years, a director will leave systems and a culture in place. You will have built several buildings. You will be well-known and loved in the churches.

After 30 years, your pathway will become a paved road for those behind you to walk on. You will leave a legacy that will be talked about long into the future.

Whether one leaves fingerprints or creates a paved road, God must get the glory for all our efforts. An institution that pounds its own chest is one heartbeat away from a heart attack. Institutions that are driven by the Spirit of God can continue to influence until He returns.

To God Be the Glory, for the Great Things HE has done! Now you go and be the instrument that HE uses for His Glory; be all you could be!

## *Points to Ponder*

1. What will it take to commit myself to this organization for a life-time of ministry?

2. Do I want to leave behind fingerprints or create a road for others to follow?

3. What will I need to do to develop the resolve needed to remain faithful for countless years?

4. How do I stay consistent and focused for 30 years?

5. How will God be glorified from my efforts?

*Not that I have already obtained all this,*
*or have already arrived at my goal,*
*but I press on to take hold of that for which*
*Christ Jesus took hold of me.*

*Philippians 3:12*

# About The Author

The author has spent his entire adult life working in a camp a-long-side of his wife, DeDe, and their four children. He is now the proud grandparent of 12; he prays too that each grandchild will have their personal "encounter" with the Almighty while at camp.

To contact the author email him at:
*earldtaylor@yahoo.com*

33145500R00137

Made in the USA
Lexington, KY
15 June 2014